Animal Lover

*One Woman's Fantastic Journey to Find Out
the Spiritual Purpose of Pets*

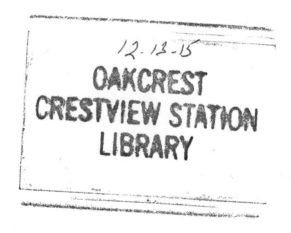
Ann Marie Hoff

ISBN: 978-0-9894716-0-2

Formatting by Polgarus Studio

Disclosure

I chose these stories from many so that you may enter more seamlessly into my story and understand as much as of what my life is like as is possible. No one who appears in these pages expected that I would remember conversations they assumed private. In respect for them I disguised names. Names are changed of both pets and people, and often, locations. People who played largely public roles are under their correct names.

PROLOGUE

"Once a thousand doors ago…"
~ Anne Sexton

If you look at a map of Iowa, and see where the point of Iowa's nose is, that's where my family farmed, only on the Illinois side of the map. When I was a child, the road that our farm lane spilled onto was called "Seven Hills Road," because there were seven hills that you could drive so fast on, your head would hit the ceiling of the car (I know this because my uncle did it routinely when his two boys and I were in the car).

Sometime in my single digit years the seven hills'were shaved down, and the moniker of the road changed to "Frog Pond Road." Not near as glamorous, and totally random, because there was no pond anywhere along our road.

After you drove out our lane to Frog Pond Road and took a left, within two miles you intersected with U.S. Route 30, which goes directly into Chicago to the east and over the Mississippi river to the west, into Iowa. During my early years, I thought the Mississippi river was the center of the entire universe. There was a 10-foot replica of the Statue of Liberty in the park on the Iowa side of the river, and I naively thought it was the real Statue of Liberty (I read a lot, but didn't talk much about the facts I learned with much of anybody, so I drew my own conclusions).

I would be nineteen before I entered Chicago, a city that was only a two-hour drive away. My main friends in those early days were the cats, calves and pigs on the family farm. I preferred cats to dolls. The first event I went to was Lassie (the dog) at the county fair in Milledgeville. I was never left with a babysitter. Instead my parents took me along for all their funeral home visits, sometimes twice a week. The funeral home would give me rain hats to play with, and my parents always introduced me as "the caboose."

As a child, I traversed the area outside the house often, picking violets for my mother, or playing farm in the front yard. I remember liking the plastic farm animals that got sprinkled with paint more than the regular ones, because they were unique. I knew each plant outside, including if it was edible or not. I loved sucking the nectar out of clover blossoms, and spent hours in the fields looking for four leaf clovers. In time I developed a deep and lasting bond with the farm animals, especially cats, then cows and horses.

Several decades later, the simple statement that I was to be an animal communicator looped constantly through my head. By then I was living in Tucson, working in pharmaccuticals, enduring constant chronic pain, and was searching for relief from the throbbing in my neck and upper back. I was prescribed medication that caused me to pass out while I was driving. As a career pharmaceutical representative, I had leaned on medication as an answer to my pain. After all, it was the world I understood and believed in: modern medicine.

After a close call from passing out at the wheel, I started to grasp at straws to solve my physical pain. I promised myself I would do anything I could, and stay neutral on my beliefs until after any treatment. I tried multiple medications, Rolfing, acupuncture, past life regression, physical therapy, and even saw a Kahuna. Nothing made a permanent difference, or gave me more than a day's relief.

I signed up to do a class on being a medium with Doreen Virtue. I was not sure I even believed in mediums, but I had read *Saved by the Light*, Paul Perry's book on angels saving children from almost certain death, and Sylvia Browne's books on her being a medium. I didn't think mediumship was something I had any talent in, and certainly did not take the class to become one. My sole goal when I attended that fall weekend, years ago in Sedona, was to learn to meditate.

I had tried to meditate, but I always seemed to have a short attention span. I knew I was a "type A" personality, always on the go and prone to anxiety. A long weekend would be just the thing, I thought, to focus on my connection with the spiritual realm, and center myself. I couldn't have been more wrong.

The first day I channeled another participant's father. Because I had said that I was told, "I was going to be an animal communicator," we spent half of one day channeling animals from the other side. All 20-plus-seminar attendees sat in a big circle, and stated all the invisible animals that appeared in the center of the circle. I had 36 animals that had belonged to me come through to other people—virtually all of my horses, many cattle, cats, and of course my first dog as an adult, a gorgeous border collie called Mandy.

When I had told of my directive to be an animal communicator to *Doreen Virtue, (author of "Healing with The Angels", "Divine Guidance")* she responded, "What you resist persists." She was right. As much as I tried to ignore being an animal communicator, the more obvious it was that I was supposed to be one. More information and skills were given to me. I gained the ability to talk to angels and spirit guides. I found several missing, lost dogs. The information that the world needed to feel the connection with animals and the earth constantly blared at me. So I started on the path of being an animal communicator, an animal "psychic" if you will.

An important revelation I had about that weekend with Doreen was that I had not trained to become a communicator or medium, I was just able to do it when I tried. The ability was already there, like knowing how to ride a bike even though you never have.

When I started working as an animal communicator and intuitive medium, leaving pharmaceuticals behind, I found that there were five basic reasons a person might call an animal communicator. These were: behavior issues, medical intuitive/empathic issues, end of life decisions, missing pets, and to contact animals/people on the other side (although I would like to say it was simply because everyone wanted to get to know their pets better). Usually, however, people have a trigger that initiates a call to me.

This book is a compilation of some of the more memorable moments and clients I have had the joy of knowing, and insight into how animals think, why they do what they do, and how to have closer relationship with your fur-footed friends. In talking to pets on a daily basis, I have found that they did not come into their person's life randomly. Instead, I found—and now fully believe—that animals come with a purpose unique to each of them, and that they return to their human family time and time again.

I have a background in science, having an M.S. in Animal Science, and then spent most of my career in medical sales. If I hadn't had chronic pain, I would not have chosen this path, at least not in this way. But what I found was that modern medicine did not heal me, and did not do anything but mask symptoms. I opened up to other avenues, knowing although insurance may cover a particular treatment, it doesn't necessarily mean it'll work. The main question I have when working with a client is, "Does this make sense to you?" Because if it does, and it changes your life, do you really need a double blind study to prove it? Keep an open mind—and an open heart—as you read this book.

INTRODUCTION
ARFIE'S STORY (RURAL ILLINOIS, 1960S)

I found Arfie in an outlying cornfield on a snow filled December day. He had long matted black and white hair, and his body broken. I picked him up gently and carried him inside. It is a tribute to how young and guileless I was to have called him "Arfie." It was obvious that Arfie had been beaten badly by someone, then left in the field to die. When I found him, he was so weak and battered he no longer could walk, and I don't remember him even barking. Looking at the situation now as an adult, I do not know how Arfie came to be in that field. I found him a mile from the main road and no one came to our farm without our noticing. It was highly unusual.

Arfie lived with us a short while. Whenever my Dad would walk by him, Arfie would offer a low growl. Perhaps I was empathic already at that age, because I could feel how much it hurt and angered my dad that this happened. Up to this point, all dogs on the farm were always enamored with my father, and even though they were "family" dogs, they always ultimately belonged to him. Arfie, however, was the first dog that was mine, his loyalty being first and foremost to me. He put himself in danger by growling at my Father but I had no idea how much danger.

We all have our issues growing from a child into adulthood. My early years were very solitary—living on a farm that was a twenty minutes drive outside of town, and being many years younger than my other siblings. As such, I had camaraderie with animal that felt much deeper, and with more understanding, than I did with any humans I knew. At school, in a classroom with twelve other children, I immediately realized I did not fit in, in a very major way.

My grandmother was the one bright spot in my home life; she took the personal interest in me my working parents were too busy to give. When my grandmother died (the first death of a human I was personally close to), I didn't know how to grieve, I was only eight years old. My mother got Valium from her doctor to help us get through the funeral, and gave me several a day as well (why, exactly, I'm not sure). At the funeral, I got to sit next to my cousin David, my favorite person in the whole world. We were so happy to be together that we giggled through most of the funeral service; perhaps (in my case anyway), a heightened after-effect of the Valium my mother had given me. Later, I received a spanking for not being appropriately sad about my grandmother's death.

Previously, there had been long periods of time when I had been alone with my grandmother, and I was with her every day when she flushed handfuls of her medication down the toilet (this lack of compliance with her medical treatment could have been the cause of her early demise, I realized as an adult). I didn't feel sadness when she died, but rather a freedom that comes with being released from a human body no longer capable of functioning at optimal capacity.

Months after my grandmother's death, I was riding the bus home from school on a fine spring afternoon. It left me off at the end of our lane, with a half hour walk to the house still ahead. I marveled at the amazing cottonwood growing by the barn, and even at the barn itself. Made by the hands of my long-dead relatives, it was three stories high and held together by hand-carved wooden pegs.

Our lane rose to a slight hill at the beginning of where the farm buildings lay. Past the top of the hill, the white cattle shed was on the left, hog buildings and a corncrib to the right. Straight ahead, our house stood on the top of a knoll, with a broad sloping lawn in both front and back.

From the kitchen window you could see the big yellow school bus when it stopped on the main road, and follow a little girl walking all the way up the long straight gravel lane. Behind the house was another large yard, with a line of silver poplar trees that were flanked on one end by a Chinese elm.

A long clothesline ran between the house and the trees along the entire breadth of the house, with three lines hanging from it. The poles of the clothesline were anchored in cement, and in future years I would use them to tie 4-H calves, horses and even a few beef cattle. However, all of that was still off in the future. On this particular spring afternoon, there were pleasant breezes floating over wild flowers, young grasses and weeds. The smell of green growth was in the air. The butterflies hummed; glad to be around flowers again. It was a weekday, and I absentmindedly kicked a rock up most of the lane.

Sometimes my father would meet me at the crest of the lane, tell me what the plans were for the evening. On this particular day, I crossed over the hill and up to the house without seeing anyone. When I reached the front yard, I heard voices from behind the house. With a feeling of dread, I walked around the house, skipping my usual snack.

Some moments in our lives seem to last longer than others. When I've had horse accidents, that moment of being up in the air, not yet hurt—knowing that you will be, but not knowing exactly how bad—seemed to last for hours. These are the moments you know your life will be forever changed; a large looming wall where you thought your path led. Those moments where, if you could, you would stay forever in the instant that comes before it, and stop the cruel turn the world was taking. This was one of those moments.

From eight feet away, I saw the back of my father. He was standing near one of the clothesline poles. His belt was tied to something on the pole, a crumbled body. In his other hand was his shotgun. He had tied Arfie to the clothesline pole with his belt, and shot him. He was taking his belt off the clothesline pole, and putting it back through the belt loops on his trousers.

I shuddered, cried out and wanted to die, all at the same time. I ran forward and threw myself on Arfie's body, crying out in long hideous wails. Arfie was still warm, but his body was not moving. A moment in time was just simply horrible, and in my mind nothing could justify it happening.

I vaguely can hear my father telling me he had to shoot Arfie; he had bitten some kid. A salesman had stopped by the farm with his kid, and he had been bitten. I didn't believe this for a second. It had been a school day, and all children had to be in school. I also didn't know the boy my father named, nor did I know the man with whom the boy had supposedly come. An angry torrent of confusion entered my mind. If there were such a boy, he would have to have come from outside my school district, and been out of school for some reason. The man was supposedly a salesman yet I did not know his name or had ever met him. The real reason my father shot Arfie glared at me angrily, dark and hard in my mind. He was simply a child. My father could not stand to have an animal not love him, not being under his control. I wanted to lash out at him. But I was young—not stupid; I knew it wouldn't end well.

Arfie was my dog. I had found him. He didn't belong to my father or to my family. I fed him and nursed him back to health. He was mine, just like the cats were also mine: mainly because everyone else was too busy or didn't care to spend time with them. In a democracy, if Arfie had bitten someone, I would have been told about it, and consulted about what the outcome was to be. He was my dog, and my father had no right to take his life. It was a betrayal to me in so many ways and it was surely no democracy.

Without Arfie I did not want to go on with my life. I wanted to lie with his body and grieve forever. I had no future; I wanted nothing but my dog back alive, in my arms.

Not a patient man, my father yanked me up off of the grass, and tore Arfie from my hands. He screamed at me—how dare I be more upset with the death of a dog, a simple animal, than with the death of my beloved grandmother, his mother? He spanked me hard. He said what I heard a fair amount in those days: "Stop crying or I will really give you something to cry about." If my parents ever had any sympathy for me, I seriously doubt this would have happened. To this day, I still do not believe the story about the kid being bitten. It was obvious men had abused Arfie, but I had never seen him lash out; he respectfully growled and warned people not to come any closer.

Furthermore, I reasoned, the salesmen that called on my dad were on specific routes. They would come routinely once a week or once a month, and most of them brought me toys. The bank associate that came out to work with dad usually brought me dolls, Chatty Cathy and her pals, the real expensive ones. The "name" of the salesman who had to visit that day was completely unfamiliar to me, and he never showed up again. It smelled of a trumped up charge at the time and, to this day, it still does.

Years later, with my mom in the first throws of Alzheimer's, I asked her to recall her memories of Arfie's death. "Didn't he bite a salesman's son?" she asked me. I pounced on it. "What salesman? What son? It was a school day!" Mom retreated. What she knows of the incident is the mantra she memorized decades ago, the mantra my dad made into the truth of the situation. "A lie unchallenged will become the truth," and as a child, I simply was not powerful enough to stand up for the truth, for my truth. Now, the truth has been lost to time, and I forgave my father long ago.

One outcome of Arfie being killed was a mistaken belief that I did not deserve to own my own dog. Cats belonged to me, but the dogs, well, all dogs under that roof had to worship at the church that was my father (later, when we had a dog named Pete, my father would lie on the floor with him and say loudly, "The only one who loves me is the dog!"). A dog might spend a few minutes with me or go on an errand into town, but their loyalty to me was nil—they went off with my father as soon as he appeared.

Decades later when I started to realize my own psychic power, I had an appointment with a woman who specialized in past lives. She told me I had a spirit that was very dedicated to me, and had come in the form of a dog, then a cow that had kicked my dad and broken his leg, then had become a horse, then a dog, and now once again a horse. Not only that, she told me, this energy had been with me all but a few months for my entire life.

I believed what this intuitive woman told me. I had not told her my dad's leg had been broken by a cow. Or that I came from a dairy farm and owned horses. Statistically, I knew knowing all that information by sheer luck was not possible. It was interesting that Arfie came back in his next life as a cow—one that violently kicked and broke my father's leg. Those of you who believe the expression; "what goes around comes around" will no doubt see the irony. My father, who had carelessly and selfishly taken the life of an animal, disregarding its feelings or the feelings of the girl that loved it, had indeed received his payback.

Like a shooting star, Arfie's time was brief. But his death shaped my future relationships with pets and men. Two decades passed before I owned a dog again.

CONTENTS

BEGINNINGS

CATS ARE MY
FOUNDATION

I think I could turn and live with animals,
they are so placid and self-contained."
~ Walt Whitman

Many people define themselves as either a cat or a dog person. I will come clean; cats raised me. It seems like the minute I could walk, I was dragging a cat around. The loss of my dog as a child, coupled with the level of commitment necessary (owning a dog,) and that I thought cats were more intelligent, endeared me to the latter.

I considered myself a cat person. I felt that the loyalty of dogs was more their Achilles' heel than a plus. These beliefs were formed in part because I didn't have a dog that was totally mine until I was in my mid-twenties. If you have dogs and cats, well, according to a study published in Psychology Today, you are a dog person. In that study it was determined dog owners would take in a cat if the cat was in dire need, but a cat owner probably wouldn't adopt a dog, no matter what the circumstances.

MY CHERIE AMOUR
(RURAL ILLINOIS, 1960S) AUSPICIOUS BEGINNINGS

My first memorable animal bond was with a little cat I called Cherie. I named her after the Stevie Wonder song, "My Cherie Amour" (*"Pretty Little One That I Adore"*). Early in life I started naming animals after current songs. A longhaired brown tabby with white paws and white on her face and chest, Cherie was tiny for a farm cat, having very small bones. She made me think of what avian skeletons were like; light, compact and frail.

Kindergarten was optional for me, so Dad decided a better use of time would be to teach me to drive a tractor. That made first grade friendships more difficult because the other twelve children knew each other. I was an outsider, isolated and alone.

As soon as the school bus dropped me off each weekday at 4:30, I walked up the lane and headed for the back of the barn. There I met Cherie in a secluded spot and we commiserated. I loved the barn; the smell of the hay, the sound of the wind on the wood beams, the hidden spaces. Cherie was always in motion. She would stand on my lap, kneading it with her paws, and then anxiously walk back and forth.

Cherie and I had a non-verbal pact we kept every school day. Weekends we didn't meet. In retrospect, that was highly unusual, but it felt natural. I was more at ease with Cherie than any human. Cherie was always patiently there, always on time, always ecstatic to see me.

FERAL FARM CAT FACTS
(RURAL ILLINOIS, 1960S)

I have met many Zen masters, all of them cats. ~ *Eckhart Tolle*

Cats were my friends, my confidants, my dolls, and my peers. I wrote out their family tree; created a cat kingdom complete with royalty, named them all and even used them for my science projects.

Salesmen coming to the farm noticed the cats streaking in front of their cars had clothes on. I found cats in clothes were so much more fun than lifeless, plastic dolls.

Cats look comical in dresses, their waist sits just behind their front legs and the full skirt flounces straight out instead of covering their bodies like on a human. The hardest thing was getting their little elbows through the sleeves. They protested at first, but generally gave in. Then once they had had enough of the doll treatment, they flounced away.

After *several* sales men commented about the cat's fashion wear, my father told me quietly to quit dressing the cats. He was nice about it, but he said people could get the wrong idea. (What idea would that be? Those Hoff Farm Felines *felt the need to be styling?*)

Another aspect of my cat responsibilities was to mobilize the mouse brigade when Dad was grinding ear corn. Grinding consisted of parking a feed grinder powered by a tractor outside the ear corn bin, then shoveling ear corn from the bin into the grinder. When my dad did this, the mice that were in the ear corn ran out. I was at the opening of the bin, with my best mousers lined up in a row to have them help me catch the mice that ran out of the dwindling corn pile. I was queasy, scared of mice, but I bucked up to help my felines. Meanwhile, they hunted the mice with skill and enthusiasm.

Each summer, I held a survival school for kittens. Classes included: climbing trees, being lost in the weeds and space flight (which consisted of spinning 360 degrees in a clothespin bag attached to the clothesline). I learned that cats always climb *up* trees, not down, going as high as was comfortable, then panic; crying loudly. Many kittens stay where they had been placed (this makes sense when you consider that when a kitten's mother puts them somewhere she expects them to stay until she returns).

There was nothing I could do to the cats that would make them avoid me: not spinning them on their sides in circles, dressing them in clothes or giving them antibiotic shots. In return, despite any objectionable behavior, like violently scratching me or eating rodents in front of me, they still had me at "meow."

I was a student of veterinary science for my cats; which was the only health plan they had. When they had infected eyes, respiratory infections, or a torn throat from a battle with a rat, I doctored them. We had antibiotics, painkillers, and other medications on the farm, and I learned very quickly how to use them. As a livestock farm, the rule was you could only call the vet for the animals that were sold for money. This translated to mean "not the cats".

If the Vet had come to see a cow, I could fudge and quickly ask him a health issue about a cat I was worried about. When I was milking cows, I noticed that a tomcat named Garfield had a growth from his ear that looked like half a head of cauliflower; seriously, the growth was the size of a small rose and as pink; it was the exact color of his inner ear.

I was sure it was cancer, because what else would look like that? I loved this cat too, and wanted to take good care of him.

After the vet finished what he came to the farm for, I asked him if he would see Garfield. He said "yes" and I scrambled off to find the cat. I couldn't. I looked in all the cat haunts; he wasn't in any of them. I had to tell the vet to go, that I couldn't Garfield for him to treat.

Then, later that night when I was milking, Dad walked through the milking parlor. I asked him about Garfield, and his cauliflower ear. He knew immediately which cat I was talking about.

"Oh that," he said, "I took the pliers and pulled that growth out. It didn't even bleed! Apparently it was totally on the exterior of his head."

I was astonished. I had spent a sleepless week thinking that Garfield had a brain tumor that filled his head intertwining with brain tissue, and that it was coming out of his ear because there was no more room inside his skull. After I got over the shock, I was happy that Garfield's health wasn't in jeopardy. This was an example of the medical training I received from my father.

The milk house where we had the bulk tank and milker sanitizing equipment was off limits to cats. Soapy water whooshing through the glass milk pipeline was loud, and the room smelled like bleach. If a cat meandered in, Dad would scare it dramatically by yowling and making screeching meows while holding it above the water in the sanitation tank. My father got a perverse pleasure in scaring cats. All were afraid of the sanitizer. I hate to say it but Dad and I bonded over terrorizing those cats.

My cats listened when, at fifteen I didn't get asked to the senior prom. They pranced and purred indicating that it didn't matter to them. When my heart was broken, or was betrayed, I explained it to them. They listened to it all, and were unconcerned. Soon, they taught me that I didn't need to make such a big deal about it either.

My feline loves caused me to stretch myself. For my cats, I was selfless. I did not judge them for killing other beings, eating meat, playing with their food in a way that seemed cruel, being dirty, getting hurt, not taking care of themselves, or getting sick and leaving their kittens to certain death. I cared for them as best I could. I took in orphaned kittens, fed them with an eyedropper, then with bread and milk. Cats were my family.

BIRD HUNTING
(RURAL ILLINOIS, 1960S)

"If you hold a cat by the tail, you learn things
you cannot learn any other way."
~ *Mark Twain*

A particularly gruesome activity I participated in for my cats was shooting sparrows at night. My father believed that birds carried disease, and he didn't like birds hanging out in and around the barn rafters, seeking shelter. His solution was to have my brother and I hunt sparrows at night. My brother had a BB gun (later a pellet gun), and a flashlight. I had a pail. I was five when this started, but it never got any easier.

After dark, with the cattle settled in the barn for the night, the sparrows were in the rafters above, sleeping too. They lined up next to each other, with their head tucked down and folded into their wing. My brother would shine the flashlight on birds that were transfixed by light blindness.

Pop! The sparrow would get hit by a BB, and fall to the ground.

My job was to pick up the wounded or dead birds, and throw them into a deep plastic pail. I choked down my gag reflex as I gathered torn apart, bloody birds. We'd work for what seemed like hours. Some birds barely wounded, hopped from of the bucket and tried to escape. I'd pursue them and toss them back in.

The pay off for me came when we were done. I would unceremoniously dump the cluster of bloody birds on the floor of the barn. The freshly killed birds were desirable morsels. The whole cat colony would all come running when I called "kitty, kitty".

FRESH MILK
(RURAL ILLINOIS, 1960-1980'S)

On the farm I got to observe cats living in their own colonies. The farm's main colony was upstairs in the barn, and fractured groups made satellite buildings their homes. Felines have lived on dairy farms for centuries, providing friendship, drinking milk and controlling rodents.

Twice a day, after milking we drained the milk house pipeline and gave the warm milk to the cats. Many nutritionists today discourage feeding cow's milk to cats, but my memories are of the cats loving it.

During milking, the milkers pulsated milk out of the udders, and the milk flowed into the glass pipelines, white, clean, frothy and warm. Fresh milk is completely different from pasteurized. It is amazingly sweet and warm.

Afterwards the remaining milk in the pipeline was drained into a bowl, so we could set the system for sanitizing. I would carry the bowl outside, up to the cement slab over the reservoir, calling "here kitty, kitty, kitty," in a high-pitched auctioneer-like voice. Excited cats would come running from all directions scrambling to partake in a family style drink fest.

COLUMBUS THE FARM CAT
(RURAL ILLINOIS1960S)

Each year brought me the thrill of anticipation of spring. Tulips, sprung out of the soil like beautifully wrapped presents. Rye grass grew overnight (we planted it to pasture the cows in spring and fall before we planted corn) rich, green and new. I could smell the richness of the deep loam soil wafting through the air. The seed catalogs that we had poured over all winter finally sent the seeds we had ordered, and when they arrived, we set about planting our half-acre garden. But I loved spring because it meant kittens.

Almost all feral mothers hide their kittens away, but the tame ones would present their family when they felt the kittens were grown enough, usually when their eyes opened while they were still blue. If we found an early nest of young kittens we'd look but not touch, for if the mother smelled our presence, she'd relocate them.

Two tortoiseshell kittens appeared in the eastside of the barn basement where Mom and I worked with the farrowing sows. Since I had just learned who discovered America, I named one of them Christopher, and the other Columbus.

Christopher died within a year, but Columbus lived well into her late twenties, becoming the farm cat matriarch. A black tortoiseshell she had salt and peppered black and orange hair with white paws. A genuine joy, she was a good friend of mine for many years.

Columbus almost wasn't our farm cat. The neighboring farm had a rodent problem and had no cats. When I was eight, the cats were considered mine, so our neighbor paid me five dollars (a dollar for each cat) to take Columbus with a litter of four kittens **to his farm**. The theory was she would stay on his farm because she had the babies.

The next night it rained and froze ice on the trees, followed by snow. Then it got warm enough to make all the dirt roads a muddy soupy mess. The neighbor's farm was three miles away by a dirt lane, five miles if you took the paved road. Columbus knew she was taking the muddy lane, even though she had been driven to the neighbors by the paved road.

By the next nightfall, Columbus and all four kittens were safely tucked into our barn. She walked the three miles; four times each time carrying a kitten in her mouth, until all of her brood was safe. She knew where home was. It was incredible to watch her, this determined mother, lifting her offspring high in the air by the nape of the neck, keeping them out of the mud. None of them got sick from their spring excursion.

My mother wouldn't allow a cat in the house, so I was always trying to sneak one in. I interpreted Mom's rule as "cats couldn't be on the floor" in the house. Our farmhouse had been built when outhouses were still in use (when we remodeled, there were newspapers in the walls with stories about the civil war). The bathroom had originally been a hallway.

Columbus combined her two passions, (love of humans and being a mother) by having babies in my mother's closet for a total of three litters. This would not seem so exceptional unless you knew how my mother felt about cats being in the house.

Columbus knew how to open the closet door, and make a comfortable nest out of Mom's clothes on the floor (we all had clothes in the bathroom so we could put on our "chore clothes" to go directly outside). Then, she'd proceed to have kittens. It turned out that that despite her distaste for the matter; my mother was too much of a softie to kick a cat with young kittens out on the street. We'd move the kittens outside once their eyes opened, and they played on the back steps for the rest of the summer.

Columbus bereft without a family. It was obvious she defined herself as a mother. One spring, Columbus's kittens were stillborn. Instead of sitting out the spring kitten-less, Columbus stole a litter from another cat. We had to find the missing mother and return them, because Columbus didn't have any milk so kittens with her would starve.

Columbus caught mice and dropped them, still alive, on the concrete reservoir slab where the young kittens hung out. Then she'd show the surrounding kittens how to play with and then eat a mouse. Next she would take kittens from several mothers and line them up to hunt for more mice.

She'd sit them in a straight line, looking at the wall of the corncrib for hours. If a kitten strayed, Columbus swatted it with her paw. When the mice moved between the ears inside the corncrib, Columbus taught the kittens how to grab a mouse's tail, and pull it out through the corncrib slats for a nutritious meal.

FAITH OF A CHILD

(RURAL ILLINOIS, 1960S)

The faith of a child: the Bible says there is nothing greater. When I was a child, I believed I could talk to God. After all, people did it in the Bible, and how were we different from them? *"Jesus loves me, this I know, for the Bible tells me so."* Why wouldn't I believe that? We sang it every Sunday.

I remember when I quit asking God for things, at least, in the "everyday" sense of it. Talking to God was the most natural thing to do, like he was my best friend that didn't want to hang out with anyone but me. Our farm went as far as I could walk. Because of location, and the fact that my brother and sister were both more than a decade older than me, I mainly played alone—except for God. Years later, I was told that I couldn't totally let go of the property, because it was where I had built things with God.

It wasn't all play. I had to help my dad sometimes. A self-made man of German descent, my father worked constantly. I was sent along to help. I was old enough to know that there were things God didn't want us to do, but I didn't understand most of them. When my mom would bow her head in church and ask to be forgiven for her sins that she had done that week, it left me confused. I knew I hadn't done anything wrong that God would be angry at. After all he talked to me all the time, and wouldn't he tell me if he was mad? To be on the safe side, I memorized the Ten Commandments. My father took God's name in vain a lot, and every time he did I silently asked God to forgive him.

On September 26th (my dad's birthday), I was assigned to help him rebuild a hog house. The hog pen had three houses, all in different states of disrepair that constantly needed to be maintained.

We were working in the machine shed, cutting wood and materials to add to the building. Dad was in a horrible mood, swearing and complaining about the fact that it was raining. He was breaking the "taking God's name in vain" commandment so frequently I was worried what would happen to him. Plus, being his birthday, I just wanted him to be happy.

September was late in the year for rain to help the crops, but I still knew it was a necessary part of life. I didn't think I should interfere to the point that it stopped raining all together. Instead, I asked God to give me the gift of the rain stopping only when my father walked outside. We were working in the machine shed, but we had to walk outside to put the boards up on the hog building. I figured if Dad didn't get wet, he wouldn't be angry anymore.

Since God and I were tight, it quit raining each time when Dad walked outside. Fifteen times straight.

It was a miracle or at least, a profound reason for Dad to be in a better mood and quit swearing. Problem was, my dad didn't even notice. I am not sure why this had such an impact on me, but I was devastated.

Actually, I was too young to realize that Dad was lost in his own black mood so deep that he no longer was aware of what was happening around him. I just knew that my gift to him wasn't important, that it made no difference if it was raining or not. The fact that it had been raining already had ruined my dad's day for the whole day, even if it didn't inconvenience him in any way.

I was thrilled that God had actually granted my wish, that it quit raining when dad walked outside. It a miracle, and my dad hadn't even noticed. I was distraught—what good was being able to change the circumstances by asking God if it didn't make anybody any happier? It was then that I made the decision to never ask God for anything again.

Oh, I did say prayers and ask for things in that whiny, complaining sort of way, but never again did I ask God for a favor like I was asking my best friend to give me a ride home. I made the decision that it wasn't worth anything if it didn't change the outcome. Looking back now, I am amazed that my dad's behavior could affect my relationship with God in such a dramatic and life altering way.

God never went away. I turned my back on him. Being raised in a dysfunctional household, I had already picked up that controlling the environment, i.e. "don't have anything happen to make Dad mad" was the only way to keep from getting abused. That day, I realized God could not help me in that. In those years, I felt dramatically alone, like I was being submerged in water where everything moved in a slow, nightmarish way, as I systematically eliminated my options. I had also come to realize that my mother wasn't on my side either. No, I was alone, and it seemed there was an impenetrable bubble over my family that prevented anyone from reaching inside and stopping the tempest that was my father.

A CALF'S BIRTHDAY PARTY

(RURAL ILLINOIS, 1960S)

Growing up, I was very
lonely. There were no

children my age within a ten-mile radius of the farm, and my decade plus
older brother and sister had little in common with a younger sibling who
was sick all the time.

I learned to entertain myself, to read, to create. I loved the corncrib,
where different grains and feeds were stored. The different textures,

contrasting colors, shapes and sizes, the packaged feeds, ground corn, shelled corn, ear corn, oats; a plethora of potential creations. I started making cakes out of shelled corn, pig starter and oats. Milk replacer sprinkled on top looked just like powdered sugar. I loved how the cakes looked. When I gave them to the baby Holstein calves they devoured them with relish.

I decided to have a birthday party for my calf. Dairy cattle have a baby calf every year. We would let the calves nurse for their first meal, or give them colostrum we had frozen for the event, unfrozen and funneled into glass pop bottles. Colostrum is the first milk after the calf is born. It is high in antibodies, protein and nutrients. Colostrum needs to be given to a calf within twelve hours of birth to acheive the highest antibody levels.

On our farm, we tied the calves with twine to trees and fences around the barn for the first several days of life. Out of these calves, my parents would give me one to be "my special calf" that I could play with, ride like a horse or dress up. (I really wanted a horse, so my parents gave me a baby calf to appease me.)

It definitely wasn't the calf's birthday; a year old the calf would have already been in the yearling heifer herd. It was more because I *wanted* a party and an occasion to show off my gorgeous feed cake making ability.

In a photograph of this party, there are five girls around a calf, all with party hats and noisemakers. Everyone has a smile. A Holstein calf is in a red and white nose banded halter at the center of the photo. The girls have party dresses on, the kind that you only see on youngsters. They also have on party shoes, with little white lace anklets. I am holding the lead rope of the calf, (through all these years I do not remember her name) and smiling. I thought my first foray into home entertaining was a success. The memory of the party is a happy one. We had two cakes: one for the calf, and one for the girls.

At school the next day, I walked up to a cluster of children, excited to share the memory of a great time. When I was within earshot, I heard someone make a comment: "Who is so weird they would have a birthday party for a calf?"

I was stunned. It had never occurred to me that the party might not be a "cool" idea. Everyone invited had come, without one word about it being a "bad idea".

I felt so betrayed. That these girls would accept my hospitality, and then talk about me behind my back! I was made the brunt of a joke. It became the most conscious defining moment of my young life.

In that moment, I promised myself I would never stick out from the crowd again. I realized I couldn't trust my own instincts, that the love I had for my calf was not something to be shared. After that day, I always watched others to make sure I was "fitting in." Decades later, I was still looking to others for what fashions to wear, what slang words to say, what was appropriate and what was not.

I wish I could say that I've since grown out of this habit, but unfortunately I am still unearthing my true self from the one I began to create that day.

This experience also initiated a cascade of events still in motion today. I kept recreating getting betrayed for the next several decades of my life. I would go out of my way to find people I could trust, only to have them somehow not be trust-worthy. It got old and tiresome, yet I couldn't seem to break the behavior.

It wasn't until sometime in 2002, that I talked about both this event and it's aftermath to my Kahuna. This was truly a godsend, because she held the keys to escape from my prison of betrayal I had created. She had access to the Akashic records (a Universal documentation of all events throughout history), and viewed the actual events in her head. I had forgotten how strict my father was, and the fact that he hadn't allowed me to invite boys to the party.

When I had walked up to friends that day after the party, the girls had been telling the boys about the event. Embarrassed to not be invited, a boy had covered with a joke. I had come in at exactly the wrong moment. I had never been the brunt of the horrible joke I thought I was. Unfortunately, though, it didn't matter because I made it real in my mind.

FIRST GRADE & 4-H

(RURAL ILLINOIS, 1960S)

First grade brought a sharp change from being the youngest child (my brother and sister are eleven and thirteen years older than me, respectively, and my sister left home when I was 5) on our farm. Kindergarten was optional in those days, and my dad decided to teach me how to drive a tractor instead of going to school that year. In first grade, the other twelve kids had already been together for a year.

My mom taught me to read at an early age, so I was already reading on my own by first grade. My parents had me so conned that they would buy me math workbooks as rewards for good behavior. In those first two years of school, I had multiple respiratory illnesses and was hospitalized eight times. One year I was in the hospital over Christmas and New Year's Eve.

Because of these illnesses, I missed more days of first and second grade than I attended. My parents brought my schoolwork home, and I finished with straight A's. In fact, it wasn't until I went to junior high and had to take PE that I received a B. (Mental learning has always been easy for me, which served me well when I started working on the farm five or six hours a day and going to school.) When I did go to grade school, I was out of the loop, I didn't know the catch phrases that were popular, and wasn't able to trick or treat in the cold October air like the other children.

In third grade, a personality test was given at school; I was the only one to show up as a "bohemian," a word that I didn't understand. When the teacher polled the class about what we wanted as a career, I was the only girl who didn't say stewardess or nurse. I wasn't sure what I wanted to be, but I did know that I didn't want to enter a profession that only girls did.

I was nine years old when I entered 4-H, and started interacting with kids other than the ones in my classroom. 4-H held a meeting once a month. We would go on field trips to businesses, hold public speaking contests, and of course, there was the county fair.

It was then that it started happening. I would be talking to my mom about somebody in 4-H, how I didn't like them and I'd get these tingly type feelings in my stomach. I thought my conscience had triggered the sensations because I was gossiping; something that everyone felt. But I never spoke about it, until years later when I worked with one of my intuitive teachers. She said; "Not everybody has that."

The sensations are like a homing device that zeros in on bad behavior. The tingles come like an alarm when I lie or even speak inaccurately.

During my teens and early twenties, whenever I felt the alarm in my stomach, I would talk louder; get pushy and demanding, trying to force away the tingles. Now I use the tingling to confirm what is going on without having to give in. The sensation occurs less frequently because, quite simply, I don't talk about people like I did when I was younger; which was the primary reason for it. If I do feel the familiar sensation, I know immediately I need to back off because I am not on solid ground.

MILKING COWS

(RURAL ILLINOIS, 1970S)

*Seva Foundation (an international aid organization), in alliance with a
Guatemalan NGO, had provided goats and sheep to give [some] women and
their children, who were not really strong enough to replace the men at growing
corn, their source of food and livelihood. And when we visited villages to which
the animals had been given only a few short years before, we found that the
project was working. The children were healthy from the goat milk; there was
meat and a little money from the sale of baby goats and sheep. What we hadn't
expected, however, was that these bumptious animals, which the women and
older children held on ropes to display to us, brought them more than physical
survival. They brought laughter and joy.*
~ Ram Dass and Mirabai Bush, "Compassion in Action"

Once I was taught to milk
cows, it soon became my
job. I apprenticed with my brother for a year, and then when I was twelve,
my brother left the farm. I milked our herd by myself, twice a day. I got up
at 5:30 each morning, milked for several hours, went to school, came home
and repeated the process again. I loved the dairy cattle, and knew that there
were many other chores on the farm that I would not enjoy nearly as much.

Because I operated the entire milking process myself, I learned creative ways to solve problems. If I had to find my father to help me because a cow was not in a stanchion, or if I got kicked, or was afraid of a cow, it would take at least an extra half hour to unhook the equipment, (get my father), deal with the issue and proceed.

The interesting thing was that cows that didn't like me, would like my brother, or my Dad, very few cows were outlaws to all of us. It is documented that cows give more milk for some people than others, and the atmosphere in the parlor was palpably changed when my father walked in the door. The cows would get incredibly tense and poop when he entered when I was milking, which of course, I had to clean up. It seemed the cows functioned as one unit; if one of them were upset they all became upset.

I simply did not have the time to go for help, so I learned early on to be self-sufficient. The experience taught me to solve my own problems, rely on myself, and keep going no matter what else went on.

I milked every morning, regardless of how I felt, whether during a blizzard, or the temperature outside was 20 below zero. When it was that cold, you had to run hot water on the milkers to keep them working. The udder of each cow had to be wiped dry before they headed out the door so they didn't get frostbite.

I usually felt good when I finished milking in the morning, I had a sense of accomplishment. I also used that time to organize the rest of the day in my mind. Furthermore my parents gave me a certain amount of respect for working so hard each day. They also trusted me when it came time to go out for social events, since I was receiving straight A's in school (except for PE) and handling all of my duties at home. Fortunately, schoolwork always came easy for me. I completed my assignments during classes, and then took a last period study hall that I skipped so I could get home for chores an hour earlier.

The milking process was magnificent to me. Even when I think of it now, I feel the radiance of the happiness it created for me. The "thu-ump thu-ump" of the milkers, and the flow of the white clean milk through the glass pipeline that carried it to the bulk tank in the next room. The parlor was what is called a ten stall run through, and five cows would be getting milked while the five next to them would be getting their udders cleaned with iodine water, the feeder in front of them filled with a crushed corn and protein mixture that was nutritious and enticing. At least one cat would walk the cement ledge behind the stanchions, where three buckets of Iodine water with large clean sponges were ready to clean udders. Two space heaters hung above the shelf, at face level, blasting heat into the cozy space.

A series of strings hung above the stanchions were the cattle stood, one that opened the stanchion, one that closed them and one that pulled the lever on the feeders in front of the cattle to give them more feed. Among the plethora of sounds was the munching of the cattle, the click-click of the feeders, the mechanical sound of the stanchions locking, and the "whiz-whiz" of the electric doors opening and closing.

When the cows became unruly, wouldn't stand in a stanchion, kicked the milkers off or even worse, kicked so badly that I couldn't put a milker on, the radio was shut off, and then as if on cue, the cows would defecate in unison. One of the first hurdles I had to clear when I started milking was to get over any trepidation of being around excrement.

I learned to walk safely amongst these one-ton milk cows, how to put my hand on their back when I changed a milker so that they didn't startle, and how to approach from the correct angle to avoid getting kicked. Even though these were extremely large animals, I came to a place where I had absolutely no fear when working with them. I was happy and joyous milking. I felted grounded when I was busy in the milking parlor.

There was a distinct rhythm to milking. The electric milkers pulsated and the cows ate, while I washed the udders on the next five cows. When the cow was done milking, I would switch the milker, and let the cow that was done milking out through the electronic out door. Then fresh cows were let in thru the in door to fill those empty stanchions. Then again milkers were changed, cows let out, more cows brought in from outside in the holding pen, and all was right with the world.

BECOMING

THE HOG TANK

(RURAL ILLINOIS, 1960S)

My father always came up with horrendous jobs for me that an adult would've flatly refused. Especially in the summer, when long, school-less days stretched out in front of me. These jobs usually either scared or bored me, and as such, consistently ended badly.

One summer, my job was to watch the hogs so they didn't jump into their water tank and drown. A cool thing about this tank was that goldfish lived in it. They were put in to eat the algae and keep the water clean.

Hogs can't sweat (they are without sweat glands). That is why they are associated with mud, which they get into to help disperse the heat and keep cool. In the summer when it got really hot, we would clip misters on the fences so the hogs could stand under the water, happily reveling in their own little water park.

Unfortunately it wasn't always that idyllic. At times, there were too many hogs, and they would push and shove to get under the coolest part of the water. The hogs that didn't get to stand in the cool misters would become hot, cranky, and desperate. This led to the occasional pig getting really hot and jumping into the water tank. Then the pig sank like a stone.

That was when my job came in; I'd have to grab the pig by the ears and try to pull it out. These weren't small pigs (they were at least a fifty pounds) so I had to use whatever leverage I could to try to drag it out to safety.

It was so incredibly boring waiting for hogs to get hot, perhaps slower than the proverbial, "watching paint dry". I couldn't help but wander off, following a cat that sauntered by, or amuse myself by exploring the plants and flowers nearby.

One day turned out distinctly different. The hog tank was located west of the corncrib. I wandered to the north, and then heard splashing and pigs squealing. I ran back to find a pig floating, dead in the water, and another trying to jump in.

I had to tell my father that I messed up. Of course he became angry. I had recently found out that the hogs we raised were sold for meat, and that they were all going to go to the slaughterhouse to die. So I sassed back saying, "What do you care? They're going to die anyway!"

I was seven years old when I learned about the eventual fate of these and other farm animals, and it shocked me. I was still too young to understand concept of money and the need for income. Although my parents paid for watching the hog tank, it went into a savings account that I couldn't withdraw from. I didn't comprehend that we raised these animals to create an income from selling them.

Although my father, in similar situations, furnace blasted me with obscenities and blame, this time he didn't. I distinctly remember what he said to me, and I've carried it with me all these years: "Everything dies. You and I are going to die some day. Our job on this farm is to raise our livestock to be as happy and healthy as possible and to make sure that they have the best life they possibly can until that day comes."

My father believed that every animal had its right to live a happy life, and that suffering was optional. That is why he did not sell the male suckling calves for veal; instead he raised them to adults. Veal calves aren't allowed to consume anything but milk. Most are raised in crates, never touching the ground. Instead, we took our male calves and raised them to full size, finishing them in our eighty-acre timber (the timber was on sand hills next to the Mississippi river. It contained a combination of pastureland and trees, but wasn't the quality soil to raise corn).

I embraced this edification from my father, and began to view the farm as a modified Noah's Ark, benefiting the animals. My family and I were caretakers and stewards, responsible for the health and comfort of our farm's beings.

MY FATHER'S GIFTS

(RURAL ILLINOIS (1970'S–1980'S)

You are never given a wish without also
being given the power to make it come true.
~ *Richard Bach*

I had two horses during my teenage years, and they were stalled at the top of the knoll that entered the farm buildings. At night when I checked my horses, I walked past the vapor light across from the corncrib, the hog pens and the confinement hog housing to my left.

I heard the comforting chirp of crickets, the bang-bang of the hog feeders as pigs ate, and their woofing as they ran away. I listened to the farm breathing, each animal, as a collective, the well being of all, a palpable presence. The labor was done for the day, and everyone was well, everything harmonious.

It was my father that instilled in me a deep and abiding relationship with animals. He taught me the notion of stewardship over our animals; that we truly were the guardians of those lives. We needed to use the most up to date medicines, best practices, and provide our animals with an environment in which they could flourish.

I am reminded of the dry cattle herd that grazed the timber. I counted them twice a day in the summers and checked to see if they were okay. They had a much richer existence than the cattle that stayed in pens all year and an incredibly more comfortable life than the dairy cattle of today's herds in Arizona and California. The astonishing fact is that the cows in herds today average only two and a half years in production. In contrast, my dad sold my cow Sunny (I was in third grade when I purchased her and named her Sunbonnet) when I was 29.

When I was in college, our swine herd had an outbreak of a major virus, pseudorabies. It was so virulent that it killed 250 pigs on the first day. In Illinois, it was illegal to vaccinate against pseudorabies: you were just supposed to let the disease run its course. This forced you to helplessly watch as the animals died and then start over seven years later (the virus stayed in the soil for seven years).

However in Wisconsin, farmers were allowed to vaccinate. My father couldn't stand the thought of helplessly watching our entire swine herd die, so he drove all night to Wisconsin and got the vaccine. In the long run it was a financial mistake; we were still vaccinating for the disease a decade later.

In his way, my father modeled how to conduct business, and how to love: you didn't just give up you fought. His was unconventional out of the box thinking, even if it meant breaking the law (I remember several heated phone discussions with my father saying; "I am not going to go to jail for saving my own animals.")

The last Christmas I spent with my father, he was inconsolable there was no longer any livestock on the farm. Close to tears, he kept repeating that it "wasn't a farm" without livestock". (Many farmers make a living as grain farmers it is perfectly respectable. In fact, that is what my brother is doing with our farm today). The thought of all the empty buildings was unbearable for Dad. (The combination of lack of help and low market prices had caused my parents to sell off their herds.)

Even I couldn't bear to go down to the milking parlor again—to walk through the door and see the condition of the pipeline and the equipment. Something caught in my throat when I thought of it, all I wanted was to remember it when it was vibrant and pulsing with life.

My father forged other belief systems in me, branding me with a brain tattoo. He gave me the belief that no one was above me intellectually. That may sound absurd now, but this occurred during a time when textbooks contained phrases like, "Farm people are not as intelligent overall as city dwellers." Many women could be easily bullied into thinking they did not deserve a place at the table of corporate life. He helped me realize that if I had a desire, I also had the power and ability to bring it into being. These traits have since served me well over the years.

Despite these strong character qualities my father passed on to me, almost more importantly, I learned from him who I didn't want to be. I didn't want to become like him; an out of control tumultuous tempest, exploding with anger whenever it suited him. His emotional behavior set me on a path to learn how to handle my anger differently and to discover why I had anger in the first place.

A FATEFUL FOURTH OF
JULY
(RURAL ILLINOIS, 1970S)

I think we all have a little voice inside us that will guide us...
if we shut out all the noise and clutter from our lives and
listen to that voice, it will tell us the right thing to do.
~ *Christopher Reeve, Walk the Talk*

When did I actually become an intuitive? Was it the first time something was a little off, when I knowingly talked to the first animal? Or the first time I charged for a communication session?

I cannot deny that an experience I had when I was sixteen, on our farm, was not normal. In those days, however, I needed everything to be as close to normal as possible, so I tried not to think too much about what transpired.

On a July fourth weekend, I was preparing for the evening milking. I had locked the cows over, leaving several dry cows that were close to calving locked in the pen behind the moving crowd gate. The crowd gate could be electrically moved up so I would not have to walk outside each time to get the cows to come into the milk parlor. The gate could also be lifted off the ground, so that the cows could walk under it.

Clinton, Iowa was having their big annual bash; "Riverboat Days" festival. It included a great fireworks display over the river, and I wanted to see all of it. I rushed with milking so that I could meet my friends in town. I had just purchased a medium blue Fiat 128 Sport and adored it.

When milking I was in my element. I always had to hustle to keep the five milkers running and the next five cows washed and ready. I am always asked;" didn't you have electric milkers in those days?" Yes, we did, but they weighed over twenty-five pounds, and had to be lifted to a strap that went over the cow's back and hung underneath the udder. When they were removed they had to be lifted again. All of this took considerable time.

Meanwhile I was among the cows, which meant getting pushed shoved and kicked routinely.

I made good time milking.. As I finished bringing in the last string, I swept the pen with my eyes. I lifted up the electric gate so that it was parallel to the roof over the holding pen. Then I cleaned out the parlor with the electric hose, cleaned the milkers, took them apart to be sanitized, put them in the sanitation tub, and started the washing cycle. Once I confirmed that the cycle was begun, I shut the lights off and ran up the path that led from the milking parlor to the house. A path I traveled so many times that I had memorized my footfalls.

Seven o'clock was the time that I needed to quit milking to make it to the July 4th festival, which was a good half hour before I normally finished, so I had been really cranking. I spent fifteen minutes taking a shower, dressing and putting on make-up. Then I jumped in my beautiful blue car and sped over the river to meet my friends.

It was a wonderful Fourth of July blast. After the fireworks show, I started home to make my eleven o'clock curfew. For some strange, unknown reason, my car chugged when I turned the corner from the main road onto our lane. The engine sputtered and stalled. I tried to get the engine to turn over again, but it was dead. Strange, because the car had been fine all the way home. In all my years of driving since, the only time I ever had a car quit running for no apparent reason was that Fourth of July night.

I left my car at the mouth of the farm lane, and walked the rest of the way to the house. Once inside, I promptly went to bed. The next morning, I woke up at 5:15, dressed, and was milking by half past five. The milking parlor was in the basement of the barn, and had a window that was eye level for anyone standing in the parlor, but outside, it was at ankle level. There was a parking space for the milk truck when it pulled in and loaded the milk we'd collected each day.

Looking out the parlor window I could see a scurry of people near the cement outside the garage. The night before, I had neglected to open the holding pen gate that would have let two dry cows back in with the rest of the herd. One of them had been closer to calving than I thought (my dad never kept records; we had to resort to looking for signs of a cow calving: full udder, softness at the tail head, etc.), and she had given birth during the night while I was at the Riverboat Days Festival.

The feed bunkers that made up the downhill boundary of the holding pen were installed with a design error. The slope of the cement cow pen ended without the feeders having any way to drain the manure and urine out from where the cows were held for milking. This resulted in an effluent of urine and excrement sitting on the pen side against where the feeders were. The calving cow was in the holding pen, and the calf had slipped down into that effluent and drowned. A freak accident at best, impossible is what would have been my guess. But I was wrong. It happened.

When my dad was doing a round of checking on the cattle to see if anyone was sick or had calved (70 percent of calves are born at night) he came across this tragedy. A cow standing with cleanings hanging from her, mooing softly to her drowned offspring. He became livid. With my father, nothing was ever thought of as an act of God: it always had to be someone's fault. For this dead calf, he placed the blame squarely on my shoulders.

The ordeal occurred around 9:30, so I wasn't home for him to drag me out of bed and scream at me in person. A raging maniac, he had super-human abilities when angry. He hauled the dead calf to the garage and laid it on the cement in front of where I usually parked my car.

The dead calf was hideous enough, but not quite adequate for my father. He got a paint stick from the machine shed (they are used to mark cattle, but my father had found that they also worked well for leaving directions and notes) and with it, he wrote "you killed this" in foot-tall letters on the cement in front of my side of the garage, then drew an arrow pointing to the calf.

Since my car had broken down, I had simply opened the door to the porch and gone inside, without knowing about debacle. The next morning, I exited from the back door, again not seeing the mess in front of the garage.

My father and I never talked about any of it (The only way I knew was from overhearing my mother and the hired man talking while I was milking). Not a word about the calf's death, the accusations written on the cement, or my mistake of leaving a cow locked behind the electric gate. I told myself that I was not going to let him get under my skin with this one, that I wasn't going to acknowledge that his behavior affected me.

During my life, I tried to manage my father's anger towards me, by finding a way to react that minimized the hurt, and maximize my control. I had gone through periods of yelling back at him, not talking to him, trying to reason with him, and plotting against him with my mother. But at the time of the drowned calf incident, I was working on being an adult, showing him an unbroken pool of calm.

I did nothing about the accusations written on the cement. By the time I was done milking that morning, my mother had dragged the calf's body away from the front of the garage to a death pile that was going to be buried that day. An hour later, she was there with a pail of soapy water and a brush, scrubbing violently, on her knees putting her whole back into it (Paint stick is oil based, so it wouldn't run off of livestock when it rains). Because of this, my dad's lettering didn't come off the cement without several hours of significant scrubbing.

After I finished milking, I walked down to the end of the lane and got into my car. I turned the key. It started on the first try.

So much was going on in my life in those days that I didn't put more thought to why my car broke down that night, especially within such easy walking distance from home. In those days I had a nagging sense that I could come unglued, like the woman featured in the Guess Who song, "*Undun,*" and lose touch with reality.

With hindsight of an intuitive, I see the signs of divine intervention: there hadn't been anything wrong with the car. My spirit guides simply did not want me to witness a gruesome scene with my name on it.

RESPONSIBILITY AND CAREER PATH

(ILLINOIS, 1970'S)

My father never apologized, never admitted he was wrong. It was always someone else's mistake. Since only Mom and I lived in the house with him, he was very predictable. If he was angry with Mom, I was his best friend, and it reversed if he was angry with me. Looking back at it now as an adult, I can see how he projected his "wrong" onto my mother and me.

Brilliantly smart, with a deep love of animals, many people assumed I would become a veterinarian. What they didn't realize is that I couldn't handle the responsibility. In my early life, the vet was the reason an animal died. Dad would only call the vet after he had tried every possible measure he could think of to bring the animal back to health. The vet would then routinely do something that resulted in the animal dying within the next 24 hours. The last thing I wanted was for everything to be my fault "Why do you want to be a vet? You're always looking at someone else's animals, and they are always dying. What is good or fun about that?" my brother asked me.

Over two-thirds of newborns arrive at night. My father would walk through the cows several times in a night, checking to see if any were calving. He got so he couldn't wait for a cow to have a calf naturally; he would rouse my mother and I from a sound sleep at two a.m. and we would help him pull the calves. Pulling a calf consisted of putting chains around the calf's front legs and then attaching a (calf pulling) machine to ratchet the calf out of its mother.

Many times I watched my father fight to keep a calf alive that had been born on the brink of death. He would lift the wet, slippery body up so that fluid in the lungs could drain out, smacking the animal hard on both sides, essentially to shock it into breathing. Often this worked. Barring a birth defect, life and death looked exactly alike. Breath was the only difference. It mesmerized me, the whispering between the two.

WAKING UP TO THE BIRDS

(TUCSON 2000'S)

One morning, I woke up about four a.m. This was unusual since I had gone to bed an hour earlier. As I lay there, I heard someone call my name; Ann! Ann! Ann! The voice had sense urgency, with uplift on the last part of my name. I couldn't figure out who it was. At first I thought someone had phoned and was speaking through the answering machine. "Who would do that," I thought. It was such an odd time. The voice kept calling with even greater urgency, Ann! Ann! Ann! Ann!

I waited for the answering machine to shut off, to be able to go back to slumber. It didn't. "Ann! Ann! Ann! Ann! Ann! Ann! "A molecule of fear crept in. Was someone in my house? The answering machine should have shut off by now, the message window being only a few seconds.

I threw on a robe, and walked cautiously to the answering machine. It was off. None of the lights were on, as they would be if the phone had just taken a message. The energy in the kitchen was calm, I could tell instantly there was no one there. I heard the call still. Again I heard my name called. It seemed to come from the bedroom that I slept in. I walked back to my room, realizing that this may be a metaphysical event. When I was coming into the knowledge of my gifts, several things occurred that seemed impossible.

Once, when I awoke from a solid slumber, I couldn't see my body. It was all light. I pulled the covers over my body, and light still shone through the fabric. I simply stated to myself, "I can't handle this," and went back to sleep. Now, when I hear people talk of how we are all light, I am buoyed. I know we are all light. Because I have experienced my body being all light.

Then there was the time that an angel came, and dreams of being in heaven.

As I walked back into my bedroom, "Ann! Ann! Ann!" grew louder. I then realized that the window by my bed was ajar, and that the call was coming from outside. There, on the ledge, sat a bird calling me, or so it seemed. Never in my life had I heard a bird call sound so much like my name, repeating so consistently.

Afterwards, awake in bed, I wished I had asked this bird some questions and found out why it was calling my name. I should have gone to the back yard where the bird was and determined what the call was about. But I was tired and in a sleepy stupor, only thinking about going back to bed.

This experience was an indication of how often I have encountered the metaphysical in those days; I didn't consider it twice. As I slid the window shut I heard, "Help us. Tell our story."

During the day, I see dozens of birds in the back yard without any of them speaking my name. If it were just a bird with a call that sounded like my name, wouldn't it still be there or comeback? The book *I Heard the Owl Call My Name* (by Margaret Craven, it talks about the belief that when one hears an *owl call one's name, death is imminent)* wafted through my memory, but the details were too hazy to be compared.

A month later, I had several visitors to the kitchen window, right next to my refrigerator, where I routinely stand deciding what I am going to eat or drink first thing in the morning. The initial visitors were a duo of doves, cooing and sitting together making the shape of a heart. "There she is," they said, "she's the one, she's the one. That's her."

The next week, a hawk sat on the same tree, in the same spot. It bobbed up and down, sitting on the same branch as the doves had, which was too weak to hold him steady. The hawk too had come to see me and say hello. "There you are. There *you* are! You are the one—I wanted to see you personally."

Coincidentally, since that time two separate bobcats have walked up to that kitchen window as well, stared in at me, then padded down the drive. The first time, my two cats were lying a mere four feet away on the carport. Doreen Virtue teaches that there are no coincidences, so does the visitation from the bobcats portend something more?

What I've noticed is that many wild animals do not run from me anymore. My vibration and appearance are such that it is no longer threatening.

UPDATE: Since this I have put this experience down on paper, it has come to my attention that the voice probably was someone from the elemental kingdom, like a fairy or garden gnome. Really, their story is the story of our earth and our wildlife animals on this planet. Fairies are the angels for animals, and the elementals also take care of the plants and the ground, the actual earth.

With this book going to print, I have had the fairies bothering me daily. They have taken stuff of importance from me, like my drivers license, only to give it back to me weeks later. I had several road trips in my car, cleaned it daily, and searched everywhere for the license. Then I opened the car door one day to see my license just sitting on the passenger seat. Now I have other things missing.

The fairies tell me that to see them, people have to believe in them. For the Elementals to help us with the caretaking of the world, our recognizing them, and supporting their work is crucial. Just as in Peter Pan when Tinker

Bell needs energy, the others chant "I Believe!" In this time of global warming, GMO corn, bee killing pesticides and many world maladies, we need to BELIEVE. Belief in the elementals allows them to be at full power. Because of that fact, their addition to this book is crucial. So crucial they were constantly barraging me about the voice at the window being theirs. Realize that if we help the elementals, we also help the world, and the animals in the world. In the larger sense, we are all one, and we need to believe and be kind to all beings.

COMMUNICATION FORAY
WITH A WILD MOUSE &
TARANTULA

One night I was up late working on the computer and watching TV. Then a mouse ran toward me from underneath the magazine basket. He sat in front of me, reaching with his front paws and staring with little beady mouse eyes. I glanced innocently at him for a second, then my past fear of mice slammed into my brain, and I screamed. Patsy came running to the rescue. She picked up the mouse and killed it by repeatedly slamming it against the wall.

Watching Patsy's version of mercy killing, it dawned on me that a wild mouse just doesn't come to a human for no reason; they will generally avoid us at all costs. Yet this mouse walked confidently, though a little timidly to me, leaving his comfortable hiding place. He came directly to me, sat in front of me, and looked up at me with all the mouse intensity he could muster, front paws pushed together in a pleading position. The message that he had wanted to talk to me flitted into my mind. By then the mouse was dead. What could I do now? I gave God a very heartfelt apology explaining that I didn't find out what the mouse wanted to share before it was too late.

FLASH FORWARD FOUR YEARS: I walked into the living room one night and noticed my dog Gracie investigating by the houseplants, her nose glued to the ground. I immediately took notice. She was watching a tarantula the size of a dinner plate, with legs that looked like some vehicle out of the movie, "Wild Wild West ". It seemed to move faster than I was capable of, even though it looked so awkward. (A vision of me bolting through the house screaming shrilly flitted thru my mind, along with the thought of getting neighborly help.)

Instead, I went to the kitchen and got a Tupperware bowl and a piece of cardboard. I flopped the bowl over the spider, then slid the cardboard underneath. I lifted up the bowl covered cardboard containing the tarantula then set him free in the desert without further thought. Little did I know that I would see this Tarantula at least fourteen more times.

When I came home the next night, the tarantula was again in the living room, hiding amidst the plants on the south wall. When I went to look at him, I saw that the vacuum cleaner sat nearby. In a light bulb moment, I had the idea to use the vacuum to suck him up. As if he could read my mind, I saw the Tarantula shudder. Then he hid beneath one of my ten-pound free weights, contorting himself as much as possible. Then the spider froze. I channeled his logic; if he didn't move, I wouldn't see him. It was pathetic really; I saw the tarantula brace, preparing for the worst. I couldn't do it. Sucking the spider up with the vacuum seemed cruel- a chicken's way out.

I really didn't know if tarantulas were harmful, so I employed the 2010 method way to find out; which was to ask people on Facebook. The resulting answers were interesting and varied. People who lived in the Midwest or the East mostly told me to kill the tarantula immediately. However, Arizonians repeatedly confirmed that tarantula's are harmless and good for the environment.

When I came home that night, there was a hairy circular button next to the outside door, on the outside wall, three to four inches across, a little more than eye level high. The tarantula was stalking me. Apparently if he couldn't find a way into the house, he wanted stay in my line of view.

I asked the guide and angels what the purpose of the tarantula was, and was told he was there to remind me of my shadow side. I was afraid of the spider and didn't want to look at him, just like I was hesitant to embrace aspects that I don't like about my personality. No matter how many times I took the spider out of the house and released him into the desert, the spider it reappeared. Like my shadow side, the tarantula was connected to me.

The lesson to me was that the longer I got used to the tarantula in my house the less I was afraid of him. (I did let the dogs in and out of the house, so apparently the spider took advantage of that. I never found another entry point that the spider could have had access to.) I saw the corollary between the spider and the shadow side; the more I looked into the darkness and understood it the less I needed to make it not a part of me or to fear it. (*See Jung, C.E., "The development of Personality"*).

The tarantula kept showing up. The last time, I had little fear of him. In fact, that time, I had a heart to heart conversation with him. I told him I lost my fear, and considering as many times as I had relocated him in the desert, his penchant for house dwelling made him look like he wanted to be a pet. If he showed again, I told him, I would cage him and find a person that wanted a tarantula as a house pet. I didn't see him again.

A full year later, while walking the dogs, I passed a tarantula speeding down the street. He was five houses from my house, yet somehow I still knew, he was headed towards my door. After walking five miles around the neighborhood, the dogs and I came home to find the spider, quietly waiting at my front door.

The tarantula did not come in, but made a plea for his story to be told. That every being, including those that really scare us, have a message for humans. All we need to do is look beyond our fear, and ask our guides what the real lesson is.

COMPREHENSION

THE BASICS OF ANIMAL COMMUNICATION
PICKING UP A VIBRATION

"A moment comes when 'other' is no longer other."
~ Ram Dass

Channeling intuitive psychic information for a client is very similar to throwing clay on the wheel in one major way; it is a feel, an experience that is hard to translate into words. Once you experience centering clay and throwing on the wheel, you never forget what that feels like. But to explain it to someone naive to the process is difficult.

I don't feel vibrations as much as I see that they are similar. I would compare it to reading sheet music instead of hearing the actual melody and beat. When I am reading for a client, it's like picking up a vibrational rope. There's a time when I've just either gotten into a session, or I've talked to one animal and I'm going to the next animal, and I'm looking for that vibrational connection. I'll fish around with questions and the guides (all of us have 30-40 spirit guides and angels. They work for us, and we need to give them direction. I use mine to help with channeling the other side) will help me get answers. The guide's work like bouncers, they let in who I want through, and keep them from stepping on each other when speaking. When I'm shifting from one being to another, there can be a few moments when I'm not totally positive who I am communication with.

I feel when I lock onto a new being. Once I get that stream that this is their vibration and energy, then I'll ask an identifying question and sometimes the answer will be no. When that happens, many times I will channel the being that is coming thru, because that spirit felt the message they had was urgent enough for them to leap frog over who I was trying to contact. Those that leapfrog to the front of the line usually have an important reason or they're just really self-centered. When this happens with dogs, they are so much about humans that the important message will be about their person. After I channel the jumper, I then go back to spirit energy that had been asked for originally.

Animals have angels and spirit guides just like humans. They are with the animal every minute of their entire lives. If the angels and guides do not shed enough light on the particular situation for me to help an animal to be free from past circumstances, I can also call on the Universe to show me the akashic records (they contain al knowledge of human experience and the history of the cosmos) on the event.

When I first started working as an animal communicator and intuitive medium, I was shocked to discover the vast documentation that exists for every minute, every second, of the lives of all beings. The guides shared with me that everyone, no matter how pure and objective they may be has a viewpoint on an event, their version of the truth (so when I ask to see a past experience, it is shown to me as a video). The version that a being remembers becomes real; because memories are created by the words and emotions that we process our experiences through. Even identical twins or littermates in the same situation will have a totally different experience of from each other, because they are running their experiences through their own brain's operating system.

If the memory is harmful to the being, or causing negative behavior issues in present time (like barking, peeing inappropriately, or being afraid of men) then I work with the angels and spirit guides to clear the energy (karma) and negative aspects of the memory. Any type of cruel or destructive action can be cleared in this way. Both cats and dogs are so open to the present moment. That move alone changes their lives.

The energy clearing will keep unfolding for several days, moving a little at a time so that there is not a harsh, stressful shift in energy. Animals that have lived lives in fear drop away the past and pick up love from those around them. It is the best single thing I can do for an animal.

THE MINDS OF DOGS

*"The gift which I am sending you is called a dog,
and is in fact the most precious and valuable possession of mankind."*
~ Theodorus Gaza

When I found out I could talk to animals, I volunteered to do animal readings at the local Humane Society's Yappy Hour. I did that and any other event I could get invited to for several years. I wanted to see exactly what my talents in intuitive ability consisted of, and get some feeling for what was normal. While I didn't limit my readings to dogs, the Humane Society Events consisted of about 90% dogs. These years gave me my confidence in working with dog intuition, and allowed me to work up a protocol. After talking to thousands of dogs, I have made some observations.

Dogs are incapable of lying. They fend off having to do so in the following ways: answering very vaguely, changing the subject, creating a diversion or leaving the room. For example, if you look at them closely, and ask them if they were the ones who nabbed the cookies off of the table, or ask if the cat was the culprit, they cannot handle the pressure of your stare. They will roll their eyes over to the corner of the room and many times follow this with getting up and barking, creating the diversion to throw you off.

My Border collie, Mandy, routinely used leaving the room version. She developed with this the "body slam". If she felt like she had done something wrong during the course of the day, when I came home from work she would physically slam into me as I came through the door and run out of the house. I would then have to look around and see what she had done so wrong that it caused her to marinate in guilt all day. Sometimes it would be something as simple as getting into an empty cat food can. Mandy had an attraction for garbage that did not die until I finally bought a dog-proof trashcan.

When I do a communication session, I haven't met the dogs so I haven't built equity with them. I have to prove I am trustworthy (if you think dogs trust all people, remember how they bark at the mailman everyday). Dogs are much more open than horses with their answers, but not nearly as diplomatic. As we know from TV advertising, however, there's a wide berth between something not quite being a lie, and total exclusion of the truth.

KENNY & THE "KISS-OFF" ANSWER

Another variation of "we can't lie" that dogs will sometime induce is the "kiss-off" answer. The first time I encountered this response from a dog was with a tiny Chihuahua. Olivia, who I knew through work, asked me to come to her mother's house and meet with several of the family's dogs. I will always remember what happened with two of them.

All of the dogs were, in fact, Chihuahuas. Some older than others, and some more grounded than others. I started by channeling Kenny, a bright dog that belonged to Jessica, Olivia's niece.

Kenny was pooping and peeing in Jessica's apartment while she was at work. When I first talked to Kenny, he was very short and curt. I asked him about the defecating issue, and he replied, "I get pissed off, angry. She leaves me alone all day. What does she expect?"

Jessica was leaving pee pads out in the kitchen, yet Kenny was defecating right by the door. I told him what Jessica expected— not to step in poop the minute she came in, but to just pick up soiled pads and throw them away. Or Kenny could wait until she came home to be taken for a walk. He didn't reply.

I went on to talk to Olivia's mother's dog, José, and had a surprise. All of a sudden, I was looking at the arm of a couch, from about two feet off the floor. The picture then took a dizzying jaunt through the whole house, like a movie that had been shot on a hand held camera. I was treated to running through the rooms and hallways—at break neck speed —staying close to the walls and turning sharply into the hall. After a disoriented minute or two, I realized that I was seeing things through José's eyes.

I hadn't asked for that perspective, but it was one of those rare times a dog shared with me their visual experience. It made me realize why my own dog, Patsy, wanted to be held so much—looking at peoples legs can get old fast. To look at a human in the face, José had to stretch his neck upward in an awkward fashion, in essence, he was saying, "Walk around in my paws, and you will see that life may be different from how you imagined."

José was well loved by his owner, and spent most of the time on the couch so both could have the same point of view. Some dogs use words, others send pictures; José was showing me his inner world. He was concerned that his (human) mother didn't get out walking and exercising enough and José had solved this problem for himself by doing laps through the rooms and hallways in the house. He also shared that he tried to make Olivia's mother laugh. A constant companion, he was aware and in tune with all the moods and feelings that his owner had. Walking, José said, would make her life much healthier and happier. She needed to get out in the sun more and walk somewhere.

After talking to José, Kenny came to me again. I could feel that he now trusted me more, seeing how I interacted with another dog. I could feel the change in his mood. He wanted to share what was really gong on with him when he was alone in the apartment all day.

"Jessica leaves, and I see her off at the door. I hear the door lock and I know that I am in alone in the rooms. I start to think about what could happen to Jessica. She could get in a car accident and be trapped inside the car, not able to come home. She could have a health issue, like a heart attack, and get taken to the hospital. Would she remember about me? Would she send someone to get me, to take care of me and feed me? Where would I go? Would they keep me here, alone, or move me to someone else's place? This is my house, I wouldn't feel okay if I didn't know where Jessica was and I was taken to some strange house."

Kenny was gathering speed and emotion with his words. I started to realize that he had obsessive-compulsive disorder. This is when thoughts constantly loop through your head, and you think of things that probably aren't true, but you can't help worrying about them. Like when you keep thinking that the oven might be on because you're wondering if you forgot to turn it off.

The condition that Kenny had was much more debilitating, I found out as he continued. "So when Jessica shuts the door, I don't know if I'm going to be alright until she comes back again. So I sit by the door, I want to know the minute she comes back. In fact, I can hear her when she walks down the hall if I am by the door. That is where I wait, right by the door. The first thing I see when she comes back is the doorknob turning. I stare at the doorknob the entire time she is gone. I don't want to miss her coming home. I am so happy to see her again, know that she is safe. I stare at the doorknob the whole day. I can't take time out to pee on the pads, they are in the kitchen, and I have to stay by the door. If Jessica is hurt, and forgets about me, how long will I be able to survive? I have food for a few days, but after that is gone, how long can I live? Will anyone remember about me? Who knows I am here? Do they care about me? Will I be left here, alone? If Jessica is in a coma or dead, am I going to die of starvation? Or thirst? I pee and poop in front of the door, because I have to be hyper-vigilant, I have to make sure I know when she comes home—I don't want to die!"

After I said most of this rant out loud, I looked around the room. There wasn't a dry eye. I could feel the fear and horror that Kenny felt, and it was one the most intense experiences I have ever channeled.

"Well, there's your answer about why he's defecating by your front door. The bigger question is how do we correct it?"

What the angels suggested was that Kenny goes to Olivia's mothers during the day, a situation that would be kind of like private dog sitting. Kenny was already familiar with Olivia's mother's dogs, a known commodity. He knew how he would be treated, and how he would act.

After that solution was applied, Kenny did not stay alone in the apartment for more than an hour at a time. During the weekdays, Jessica took Kenny to Olivia's mother's house and then kept him with her whenever possible, when she went places on the weekend. When Jessica had to go grocery shopping or run errands, she would make sure and tell him what time she would return. The added bonus of this solution was that Kenny rode in the car almost every day. He was so impressed that Jessica tried to calm him and he knew that she really loved him by coming up with this solution. Because of this, he recommitted himself to behaving, and the accidents were a thing of the past.

Like Kenny, I have found that many dogs spend a lot of time in their heads, thinking out issues. Some dogs think in what I would call "loops"— three to four sentences that keep repeating in their heads. When those sentences have a rhythm and speed to them, I have a harder time breaking into their thoughts to bring in fresh ideas, and to try to find a thread to help unravel the behavior that their owner is finding objectionable.

Dogs too, can become ungrounded (see Appendix on Grounding) and suspended in projection. Something simple like touching them on the shoulder, standing them on grass or dirt, or involving their senses will bring them into present time and out of their cyclical mental revelry. So in talking to them, I ask what their favorite toy is, what they like to eat, and what treat is the tastiest. Grounding them in such a way brings them into the here and now.

I have found that no matter what the initial reason for a session, few dogs will miss the opportunity to discuss what their favorite toy is and what they like as a treat. Dogs see this as perhaps a once in a lifetime opportunity to communicate what they really enjoy. When you put a dog at ease and start talking about their likes and dislikes, the veil of suspicion drops and they start speaking in real terms (this also works with people as well). I usually give them time and let them come to the topic on their own; if you push it, it isn't as natural. The best channeling is when I am talking for them and I don't know exactly where the topic is going, or even what the point of the sentence is. They will come to a place where they take a deep breath and release. They trust me more, and will come out with the truth. The initial response, although it isn't a lie, can be more like a, "Why should I tell you?" Some dogs need a bond with you, and the knowledge you do not mean harm to them.

THE MIND OF CATS

My first foray's into animal communication, I
volunteered to do readings at the Tucson Humane Society's Yappy Hour. I
did this because I wanted to make sure I actually could talk to animals, and
what the limits of my abilities. This gave me the opportunity to talk to many
animals, and get experience under my belt.

When I moved to a grander scale, I took ads out in pet magazines.

Because of an ad in Cat Fancy, I was inundated with numerous calls from cat owners about behavior issues and lost cats. I was shocked at the difference in personality between cats and dogs. I quickly realized that my work at the humane society had mainly been with dogs, and that cats were a totally different animal.

First of all, cats will get pissed. I have known that subconsciously for some time now, and witnessed it first hand when I was the focus of their wrath. One Christmas when I went back to Illinois for ten days, my housecats in Tucson got up on the shelves above the fireplace. They pushed every item on both shelves down to the floor, leaving piles of broken glass in an arc on the floor below. I knew then it was to show their displeasure for leaving them alone for a long length of time.

While cats cannot lie either, they can be very adapt at leaving out facts that could incriminate them. They do not have the same relationship with death that humans do, and view death more like walking from the kitchen to the living room. Many cats that their owners think are lost are fine, and consider themselves coming home someday.

I have enjoyed getting to know cats better. Of all creatures, cats have been the most constant in my life. Finding out that I could communicate telepathically has been a great gift, one I am sharing with you here.

SPIKE

One of my current cats, Spike and I argued for close to two years on whether or not he could hunt. I wanted him to kill mice and pack rats, not lizards and rabbits. In response, he declared that he either killed or didn't kill; he didn't get the gentle nuances of species.

I gave Spike "no-kill" orders. Then I noticed he had gotten fat. I blithely said to him, "Spike, you need to start hunting again, you're getting a gut!"

At dusk, (a few hours after my directive to Spike) he found a nest of baby bunnies, killing them one by one in front of me, until all four were dead. They screamed hideously, eerily similar to what human babies in pain would.

The next day I told him, *"no more hunting,"* after a sleepless night with the death cries of the baby bunnies reverberating in my ears. I thought that was the end of it.

Then Elvis came into our life. He was bright, bouncy, obnoxiously active and happy. Elvis had boundless energy, and worshipped Spike. Elvis had such a crush, that he followed Spike everywhere. When Spike stopped, so did Elvis; sitting exactly on top of him. That put a crimp in Spike's style.

I advised Spike that if he could survive the idol worship for a year, he would have the best friend he could ever imagine. Spike hunkered down and took on being an idol, a role model and a soft place for Elvis to sit down.

My neighbor visited one day. He enlightened me that Spike had been hunting at his house, during the hunting ban I had imposed on him. Spike had been catching and killing, on average, one rabbit, ground squirrel, pack rat or lizard a day, at the neighbor's house. My neighbor had never mentioned it before, bringing it up now because it had stopped. We both knew Spike could no longer catch wildlife with a rambunctious kitten following in his footsteps and sitting on him every time he stopped.

Spike understood I had told him not to kill. He still apparently liked and wanted to hunt, so he did it behind my back. While it wasn't lying, it was excluding the facts, and it's a more complicated thought process than most people usually attribute to animals.

My neighbors think Spike is the smartest cat they ever met. If you say Spike's name, he will come running to you, even if you are a total stranger. He also looks both ways for traffic before he crosses the road. If there is traffic coming, Spike will sit down and wait for it to pass.

THE ONCE AND FUTURE KING

On a break from talking to pets at an adopt-a-thon I was working for the Humane Society, I went through the adoptable cats. My cat, Speedy, had passed a few months earlier so that Spike, was currently my only cat.

The Humane Society had so many kittens they piled crates filled with them in a front room of the complex. Elvis was in a crate with his siblings, but he was the only one who walked up to the front of the crate when I was there. He had an incredible personality, very self-assured and laid back, amazing traits to have when in an orphanage. He had an adorable black spot on his check right under his nose, and even though he was black and white, had additional, randomly placed "BB" sized spots, like someone had opened up on him with a black paint gun.

Elvis fell asleep on his back on the humane society desk while I was filling out his paperwork. We put Hawaiian lei on his stomach and took his picture, and then a volunteer was waking him because it was giving her the creeps to see him lying there like he was dead. Elvis knows how to relax.

At the rescue, Elvis was given a macho name like *"Rambo"*. I threw out the name, "Mike" to him. He responded immediately with, *"You won't remember that name even seconds after I die. I want a name that befits me. I want to be known as 'Elvis.'"*

He proceeded to give me three reasons that he should have that moniker: "I have mostly black hair. I am one of a kind. And I would like to be known as *'The King.'"* *(I can't lie, that name made me wonder what I had in store for me, it was unsettling)*.

What I didn't know is that my Elvis would also become an incredible foodie, loving gravy and comfort food, just like his namesake. Plus, he was a singer and a talker. By far, Elvis is the most verbal cat that I have ever known.

A month after I had brought Elvis home, I was unpacking the ceramic plates that I make for the art fairs. One had a black and white cat on it with his tail wrapped around a red heart. When I looked at it, I gasped. The cat on the plate was Elvis. I had made it before Elvis was born. He foretold his coming, with his tail wrapped around my heart.

CONVERSATIONS WITH DOGS – WHAT'S IN A WOOF?

"If dogs talked, one of them would be president by now.
Everybody likes dogs."
~ Dean Koontz

When conversing with dogs, I often feel their difficulty in not being able to find the exact word in the human vocabulary to express their message. They'll often use words in conflicting context. However, the feelings they send me often explain the true meaning of the words they provide.

As a young boy, Mike and his Dalmatian were inseparable. When he was an adult, I reunited Mike to his dog that had long since passed to the other side. The Dalmatian came through saying, "He loved me even though I was 'stupid'. I was 'stupid' and he still had an open heart to me."

I knew by the way the dog was saying "stupid" that it meant something other than ignorant or lacking intelligence.

When I finished channeling, Mike shared with me that his dog had epileptic seizures and often fell off the porch steps shaking and foaming at the mouth. The word "stupid" was the Dalmatian's description for epilepsy. Mike shared that he had loved his dog so much, that the seizures had no relevance. Theirs had been a truly powerful relationship, that in his youth, Mike drew great strength from.

What can complicate animals' choice of words is their hesitation to say anything negative. Lets face it; you need an extensive knowledge of language to know the subtle nuances of verbiage. Dogs give me a few choice pictures and small word clusters to decipher their meaning.

Scientists have documented that an adult dog knows about the same amount of words as a young toddler. In regard to messages from canines, I get a mixture of words, feelings, and pictures (thank God I don't get smells; I don't think I could handle experiencing the extended versions of butt sniffing which dogs enjoy). The stimuli sent to me are so intertwined with each other that I have to consciously stop and think of what came first, and what exactly is being transmitted.

Information comes through to me the same way whether the beings are dogs, horses, cats or humans. From younger animals, I receive more pictures; from older animals I usually get more phrases and words, depending on how much they have lived in the company of humans. I have never had a dog come through saying: "Arf, arf…arf, arf." Apparently they know that barking is not the best way to communicate with humans, except perhaps when they have to get our attention like when someone has fallen down a well or a burglar comes to the house.

In sessions with dogs, it has often been revealed that they watch TV. I find two major reasons for that: either they want to expand their vocabulary, or they like to watch the shapes and colors move around the screen. Dogs have expressed to me that they like it when someone does an action that is paired with a word or phrase, like, "I am walking to the mailbox." The dog gets to see the person on the screen walk to the mailbox, and then gets an inkling of what walking is, and what a mailbox might be. One dog specifically told me that he did not like TV soap operas, because people just stand and talk to each other. I must admit that I had never thought of this, but it made sense.

During a session for Karen in Tampa, Florida, her dog came through very enthusiastically, saying how much he enjoyed watching the show "Speeders" with her boyfriend while she was at work. They cranked the sound up really loud, and the dog got to howl passionately along to the siren of the police cars chasing "Speeders." It was heavenly male bliss, and the male dog was quite happy to have a night of male bonding.

Some dogs ask for cartoons. They like the loud, flat shapes of color, and the vibration of the happy music that usually accompanies cartoons. Much like dogs themselves, cartoons are happy diversions to the humdrum of life. I am not saying that dogs have ADHD (attention deficit hyperactivity disorder), but they do like to be intensely involved in one thing and then switch to something totally unrelated.

One memorable dog, just 15 months old, had specific orders on how he should be spoken to. What he said was, "I don't want you to use three to four syllable words. For that matter, could you please stop using sentences? I get distracted and lose your train of thought, or whatever it is you are getting at. Sometimes four syllable words sound like a sentence and that confuses me too."

He was on a roll, so I let him continue: "What is it with the word 'understanding?' I know that 'under' means down, and 'stand' means to be up, to stand up. So that word totally confuses me, how can you be 'down' and 'standing' at the same time? I just don't get that word, quit using it! Use words like 'out,' 'down' or 'speak' for God sakes—leave having a conversation to your human friends!"

CLINTON AND NINA
(SEDONA ARIZONA, 2000'S)

Young dogs tend to send me more pictures when they communicate. When I talked to Nina, even though she was six years old, she sent mainly pictures and used very few words. It made sense when I found out she came from a puppy mill; she had very few interactions with humans in her early life.

Nina sent pictures, or video snapshots, accompanied with a feelings or emotions. When I asked for clarification a spotlight was put on the place that was significant, much like the hint light on the "Where's Elmo" pictures in books or computers.

Often, the first picture I am given by the animal only comes into relevance when I am shown the next video shot (or picture), and the feeling/emotion that accompanies it. For example, Nina sent me a picture of her in a room in a house; where there was a dog bed, blue rugs, with the room comfortably warm. Nina had a pleasant feeling in that room. Then, in my mind's eye, the picture changed, and I saw a sidewalk, with dirt on either side of it, accompanied by a panicky feeling of being unsure and unsteady. There was no security, no safe place.

From these two pictures, I easily realized that Nina was afraid and very obviously not happy when outside on the sidewalk or dirt. To make the topic even more interesting, Nina then showed me green grass and started rolling in it, scratching the grass with her back legs and running around like crazy, in an ecstatic mood. So apparently, she had a very different experience on grass than she did on dirt and cement. I was able to surmise that grass was playtime, that she was with friends and wasn't as scared.

When Nina was on cement, it usually was because she was being dragged to get health checks, shots, or was being manhandled by people in what appeared to be lab coats. Of course, all of this information that I am now sharing with you was conveyed to me in pictures and emotions. When this happens, I try to be as pure and honoring of the information as possible.

With this part of being an animal psychic having the ability to communicate with angels and spirit guides is a big plus. If I have been too off base on the information, they will provide additional input or say, "No, ask more questions."

Clinton, Pam's newest addition to her family, was a strong individual. He appeared to me as a shorthaired Doberman, and did a chest-pounding rendition of his purpose as a guard dog for his new owner. He insisted that he needed more room for exercise, and didn't like being cooped up in such a small apartment. When I shared this with Pam, she replied, "How much space does a Yorkie need?" I chortled. Clinton was posturing as a

Doberman when he was actually was a six-pound Yorkshire terrier.

I cleared the energy on both dogs, so they were comfortable in their own skin and not carrying around the reactions from their past experiences.

Pam tended to put a lot of labels on her dogs. That was the biggest risk that the fear would continue, she would again define both Nina and Clinton as "puppy mill dogs," or a hundred other monikers that would recall and reinstate past behavior. I warned Pam of this, and told her to call me in a week or so; to make sure that Clinton's energy had changed, for a better future. I've only had to clear a handful of dogs more than once, but I wanted this little soul to have the loving future he deserved. I also did my standard routine, which is to work with God and Universal law enforcement, and asked the Universe to surround both dogs with healing light.

THE WORK

LOST PETS

A pet gets lost far too often in the United States. In fact, one in three pets will get lost in their lifetime. Most of these dogs and cats do not find their way home. One in 50 cats are found, one in ten dogs. Sadly, dogs and cats get lost everyday. Many Mediums and Intuitives look for lost children or do remote viewing (looking at situations from another location psychically). Because of my connection with animals, it was a natural progression for me to look for lost animals. I have been very successful finding lost dogs, and lost cats. After finding over 800 dogs, I have learned something about the habits of pets that are on the lam.

THE MECHANICS OF LOOKING FOR A LOST PET

I have around a 90% success rate with finding lost dogs and have a 70% track record with cats. Cats and dogs differ widely when it comes to being lost, and they can disappear for totally different reasons.

Looking for a lost pet usually starts when I receive a phone call. Initially, I'll just need the name of the owner, the name of their pet and their address. This allows me to have a human connection, and through that, I have a link with the animal. This occurs because the vibrational pitch of those who love each other is connected. Think of this as a radio station signal, coming in at a specific frequency and a certain place on the dial.

From the phone connection, I usually get a visual picture of the animal, and then I ask the client if that picture is accurate. I can tell what the animal is thinking, so I know if they are in hiding or out running around on the freeway. I usually can tell what direction the pet is in comparison to where the owner is standing.

From the energy around the animal, I pick up fragments of names of streets, descriptions of their surroundings, and travel situations. In my mind's eye, I can see the path that the animal took, many times having it show up as a red line on a map, like directions from a GPS device. The client will usually be able to confirm information on how their pet left; I will pick up on environmental conditions at the time it happened (light, dark, stormy, windy, etc.). The sooner I am called in on a case, the better. For example, one dog in particular had roamed all over the neighborhood before I was contacted. When I looked at the path the dog had taken, it was as if someone had scribbled all over the map with a red crayon. I was shown where the dog had been, but couldn't distinguish were she was at that exact moment.

After that, I tune into the way an animal feels, what the animal sees, whether alive or dead, and whether or not the animal is hurting. I will scan my body to feel the dog's condition. My arms stand for the front legs, my own legs for their back legs. Immediately, I will get input such as a pain in my right leg, or soreness on my left front foot. The benefit of this information is two-fold. The first is to obtain accurate information on the dog's condition. Second, if they are in pain, thirsty, or hungry, then it's obvious that they're still alive and not in heaven. All these sensations happen when in physical form. I do not lead clients on and keep looking for a dog that I know is dead. I also can tell if there are humans with the pet.

Some dogs turn to a certain direction outside of the residence and take a straight-line journey out. When that happens, I am not sure how far they have gone—again, like looking at a GPS map without the names of the streets or a distance scale. As much information as I get, from dogs, their guides and the teams I call in; not one looks at street signs and dogs don't always follow human roads. Many of them do the exact opposite, the dogs stay off the main thoroughfares and they hide from humans. Even a very tame dog will do this for self-preservation.

In this first interaction with the clients, I put protection around the pet. Dogs and cats have spirit guides and angels just like humans do, and you can always ask for what I call "special teams."

When it comes to finding lost pets, I rely on St. Anthony, he is ideal for anything that includes the word "find;" St. Francis, who has long been associated with animals; Archangel Raphael; and also Archangel Michael.

I have honed my locating abilities by practicing with my spirit guides on other things; parking spaces, exact change and finding personal items. That builds up my trust muscle with my spirit guides, and my knowledge of how to interact with them.

Just as I do, you can ask these "special team members" to protect your pet and keep them safe, or call in those angels and guides with whom you are most comfortable (I was raised Presbyterian, but have found that the Catholic saints such as St. Anthony and St. Francis are very real and dependable).

I also call on the elementals. They are special magical beings that are associated with the earth. They help people who are connected to animals or take care of nature and the earth. It is true that you have to believe in fairies to see them and have them help you. The elementals include but are not limited to: fairies, gnomes, water spirits, elves, and leprechauns. Any time you need help with something having to do with nature, make sure you call on the elementals too. I have found that they are effective, efficient and immediate.

Dogs that have been lost for a number of days usually have a place where they have stopped running and are living in. For many dogs, this will be somewhere they can sleep and not be seen, somewhere that has access to food and water. Multitudes of these runaways have been abused sometime in their lives, so their trust of humans is fragile. A dog that knows how to be cautious and protect himself or herself is also a dog that stays alive. The last thing lost pets need to do is be out in the open getting run over, or taken advantage of by strangers.

Unfortunately not everyone is an animal lover.

As a medium, I talk to everyone (dogs, cats, people) on the other side. All mediums have a different mix of what senses come through from the other side. For me, feelings are the strongest, then words and pictures. Quite often I also get smells. Smells almost always shock me, because they are so physical and unexpected.

When I channel from the other side, I very often feel the way that spirit felt as they died. I am told it is the way they leave this world, so it is also the pathway they come through to come back.

When searching for an animal, neutrality is paramount, and the more emotionally attached I become the less effective I am. To negate that effect, I have a team that I confer with that consists of three additional Intuitives. We consult over the phone, and the only information they get about the case is the pet's name, owner's name, and address. I look to them for confirmations of my information, and it amazes me what comes forward. This also brings an infusion of new energy, information, and ideas.

If I am worried that a pet has been hurt or is dead, confirmation from another intuitive helps to believe it is probably true, enough so that I can share my fears with the clients. I walk a fine line: being as honest as possible with a client but still sharing everything that comes through. Many dogs pass information on with pictures, many times flashing one picture after another. Some of these pictures have a meaning that is immediately recognizable, like showing a trap or the fence that is broken. Others I may have no idea what they mean, or they could just be pictures of their surroundings, what they are looking at, or it may be the obstacles that are keeping them from coming home.

One of the members of my team is terrific with maps, directions, and street names. She gets on Google Earth, and we look at the path the pet took, possible locations. Since I don't get "the dog ran 2.5 miles" we often have the pet parent go way from their house, and then call. From that, I can get a hit on how far away and in what direction the animal is from the owner's new location.

Nothing is lost in God's world. While pet and owner may be physically separated, the animal's energy is still with its owner. I found a blind border collie that had been missing a month when I was contacted, and we looked for her for another month and a half. I could tell from the owner's energy on the phone that the dog was not dead; she was also only coming out at dusk and hiding the rest of the day.

A lot of people will call me as a last ditch effort. Often I get called in on a case after an animal has been missing for a good while. I also help rescue groups find lost dogs. Commonly these dogs have run away from the new "adopters," and the rescue group doesn't find out until they call to check up and see how the dog is doing. By the time that's happened, several weeks can have easily elapsed.

Once I a friend from Kansas City was visiting me, and I was doing an intuitive session for her. She casually mentioned that she had a dog that she lost several years earlier—five years previous, to be exact. It came through that the dog was living with someone else in Kansas City. We then went on to other information.

When doing a session I keep a pen and pad available to write down or doodle what comes to me. As we talked, I had some numbers come through in my mind and wrote them down. I also picked up on several words, like Clarion or Tremont. Being a medium, I get names that come into my head, but I don't know who they are or what they might refer to. If I write the name down while I am channeling other information, I can then go back to it later. My Kansas City Client looked over at the pad I had been doodling on and gasped. "That is a road that is several minutes from where I live, and those are house numbers!" When she returned to Kansas City, her dog was at the house that belonged to those street numbers.

Sometimes, the information I receive isn't too easy to pass along. I once had to tell a woman her cat had been devoured by an alligator (true story: I don't have a vivid enough imagination to be able to make this stuff up). I feel how the animal feels, what happens to them physically. Then I have to match that with my knowledge and experience. Truthfully, to tell someone that his or her animal is dead is not my idea of a good time. I want to be absolutely sure.

When I channeled a dog killed by a bullet, I knew immediately what that pain was, and will always remember how it felt. When I tell clients of a pet's demise I have asked my guides numerous questions about the situation. I also consult other Intuitives about the location and condition of the animal. One of my team locks onto an animal simply by the name. She proceeds to tell me all about the pet I am looking for with such sparse information. Everyone works a little differently, and most of us are self-taught. As a result, you become very aware of energy, how it feels, and the subtle differences in vibrations.

A tricky distinction is delineating the feel of an energy passing to the other side (how they died) from the pain they have in their body because they are in jeopardy. Even with someone that's dead, I am able to feel how he or she felt, and will feel what he or she died of.

For example, if I'm channeling someone that died of a heart attack, I will feel a pain in my heart. If somebody had liver cancer, I'll feel a pain in my liver. That also comes through with animals. When I channel energy I immediately get how it feels, and if energy aches somewhere it is a good sign because it means they are alive. A lost pet that's experiencing a lack of food or water can be in throbbing pain. Hunger, frostbite, pain, and fear can all be companions on a pet's journey home, and act as clues that someone's beloved pet is still alive.

I was ambivalent on how much to charge when looking for lost pets. It obviously takes much more time and intensity than a simple hour-long session with a client. When I start, I never know quite what I'm getting into, whether it will be a one-time session, or drag on for months. I once spent a frantic hour helping a client look for her lost cat only to discover later that day that it had been locked in an upstairs bedroom closet.

MY FIRST LOST DOG

The first dog I looked for was a border collie-Australian shepherd cross whose name was Samantha. Her owner Sandy contacted me about Samantha. Sandy had two dogs, and they both had dug under the fence and gotten out, however the older and trust worthier dog returned after a few hours.

Complicating matters was the fact that Samantha was in heat.

Not spaying or neutering your pet can have very real consequences. If you do not spay your dog, you need to make sure that they are safe when they come into heat. Hormones can be very demanding, controlling a pet's actions. Anyone who thinks this is not true has not been around cats in heat, stallions during breeding season, or bulls. On the farm, our Holstein bull knocked down five fences and traveled two miles to breed a cow in heat. Not being a responsible pet owner accounts for much suffering. If you have a reproductively functioning pet, take additional precautions and the responsibility for that.

Sandy felt guilty she had screwed up. Hers were two big dogs that she wasn't exercising consistently. Herding dogs are bred to work. Light work is eight hours a day for them. A walk barely takes the edge off.

Sandy pleaded for my help when I was in an office she worked at. I spent several days helping her look for her dog, including an Easter afternoon. What I determined was that Samantha was in a dry wash bed. We got out a map and plotted where the Sandy's house was and what washes Samantha could possibly be in. When I tuned in on Samantha, I could feel her raw throat, her thirst. Her paws hurt, so I knew Samantha was still alive.

While meditating on Samantha, I was suddenly jarred by the appearance of a gigantic woman's head. So large in fact, that nothing else was in my field of vision, except for a fading to black around the edges. My first thought I was, "What the heck?" Then it came to me that Samantha was in a hole on the side of a wash, and this woman had stuck her head down the hole to look at the dog. Personally, I never recommend doing that (you could easily be bitten). This large headed woman took pity on Samantha, and took her to the ranch where she boarded her horses. (I saw all this). I told Sandy, who identified all the horse barns around the wash.

Sandy obviously had OCD (obsessive compulsive disorder). She constantly looked for Samantha, put out flyers, and went to every horse barn that was on the wash. Sandy had fliers at Petsmart, veterinary offices, feed stores and grocery stores. After several weeks, an Asian woman called Sandy, and said that she knew who had Samantha. After seeing all the flyers, an Oriental woman wanted to put Sandy's mind to rest explaining that Samantha was safe, happy and cared for. Frantically, Sandy called me, bereft, because she had no proof of ownership.

The current home for Samantha was with the woman I had seen earlier. She had horses and a son ecstatic to have a dog pal. With the genetics of a border collie and an Australian shepherd, Samantha was a lot closer to her purpose with the kid and the horse ranch than she was sitting idle at Sandy's.

I told Sandy if she really loved Samantha as much as she said she did, she'd leave her with the new owners, where Samantha was happiest. Sandy got upset and hung up on me, and I never did find out how this story ended. Funny thing with people, they get into ownership of a dog. The reality is; you have a dog's heart or you don't, which is irrespective of whether you have physical ownership. The tried and true statement, "if you love something, set it free," was aptly true in this case.

DEBBIE'S TALE

Debbie had been lost for about a week when I was contacted. A bichon mix puppy mill refugee, Debbie had been placed with an older couple, and when she saw a chance to run away, she flew. The bichon rescue people were desperately looking for her, and Debbie had been spotted the day before, appearing bedraggled. When I honed in on Debbie, I felt a horrible stomach ache. In that split second, I decided that the stomachache was just that, and gave the rescuers the names of the cross streets where it had been shown to me that Debbie would be.

Debbie was there all right, but unfortunately her body had been ripped apart by coyotes, her stomach torn out. I had mistaken the intensity of the feelings I had channeled. I had mistaken the pathway in which she had left the world from for real time senses. Because the rescuers had called me quickly on the road, I had given them the information I had quickly without waiting to see if that was all the information.

Debbie taught me an invaluable lesson. When channeling people I could not feel them the first few hours after they passed.

Humans appear to go through some type of "life review" after death and are unavailable. What I realized with Debbie is that dog spirits are available for contact immediately. Unlike a dog in pain that drops his body and then is euphoric, Debbie had none of the euphoric vibration of heaven. In all likelihood, this was because her spirit was still earthbound.

A TALE OF GUILT & REMORSE

Searching for lost animals for years now, I've protocol that is very effective. The ability to see where dogs go, what condition they are in, and what their surroundings are is advantageous. I usually don't concern myself with why somebody has lost a pet. Occasionally, it's because of poor stewardship, and then I might not take the case.

A woman, Tara, called me from Oregon, saying she had lost a dog. But when she got into the story, it turned out that her boyfriend wanted her to get rid of the dog. A woman who had been dog sitting told Tara that she would provide a great home for the dog. When Tara followed up after giving her dog away, the sitter had passed the dog on to someone else, and wouldn't say who. Obviously this dog was not out on the street or begging in back alleys.

I tentatively agreed to help Tara on the phone. She was motivated by guilt, for having made bad decisions and for not having been there for her dog. She had broken up with the boyfriend, and felt she had given too much away while she had been with him (which included her dog).

I did a primary analysis and then called another member of the search team. After sharing the details, my team member vehemently refused to help look for this dog. I thought about it and called Tara back and said I couldn't help her. There was no lost pet, just a lapse in judgment.

BETTY FROM SMALL PAWS

There are slight differences every situation, and I gain more experience with each animal. One dog in particular, Betty, was all over the neighborhood because the searchers had waited a month before calling me. It wasn't even the owner looking for her- it was the people from the breed rescue group. They realized, in retrospect, that they had made a mistake in adopting her out. Betty was a puppy mill survivor, and she had promised herself that she would never be caged again. After she escaped her new home, Betty came back multiple times, agonizing about whether to trust her new owner. He had put a cage in the front yard and rigged it with some type of treat. This solidified Betty's resolve to leave the home, the fact that the man wanted to cage her. When I was called in on the case the dog had been everywhere. That is the problem with waiting.

PREVENTION

The best way to find lost dog is to never lose them. Prevention of loss is worth every moment, every penny you spend. A solid fenced yard is like an insurance plan. Take time to walk your fence so that you know it is solid and your fur kid will be unable to escape.

There are currently a few collars on the market that have GPS tracking in them. The technology is currently not available yet to place GPS unit into an implantable chip, but that may soon be the answer to all the grief, pain and worry of losing a pet.

PREVENTIVE MEASURES:

- Many dogs or cats run away because of something they are scared of: thunder, fireworks, or a prowling coyote. Be proactive and limit their exposure to these key triggers. Try a THUNDERSHIRT (a physical garment that hugs tight to your pet makes them feel less anxious) if you have a dog that has these fears.

- Have photos of you and your pet that are dated. When I was in my twenties, my best friend one day found his dog that had been previously stolen with some other people at the park. Of course, these people said the dog was theirs. My friend was furious but had nothing to prove the dog was his. Dated pictures with you and your pet can come in handy for proof in a situation like this. Although it isn't exactly an everyday occurrence, suffice it to say that it does happen. You want to have a fun picture of your four-legged pal anyway, right?

- If you have an unaltered pet, keep your guard up with additional precautions during seasonal breeding periods, or periods of estrus for females, and always a consideration with unaltered males.

- Get easy to read collar or tags. I use a collar where they stitch the name into it. That makes the collar easy to read when people look to find your name and phone number.

- Take the dogs for a walk in your neighborhood. They will learn the lay of the land and become familiar with the area, knowing how to get from one place to another. If they accidentally get outside and they get chased by a coyote, or choose chase the opposite sex, they might not know where they are when they stop running. Dogs are so in the moment that they don't think: "Oh, I'm leaving home and I'm not going to be able to get back." They think, "Wow, I've gotta run right now." Only later is it, "Darn, I don't know where I am; I have no idea how to get home!"

STOLEN PETS

I was very confident with finding lost pets until the fall of 2011. Then I was presented with two different dogs from two different states that had met the same fate. Hunters in the area had come across the dogs, and found them so desirable, the hunters took them home with them, ignoring the fact they belonged with other people. Both dogs were taken by vehicle out of the area, so even if the dog managed to get loose, they would be unable to quickly make their way home.

I was reminded me of a dog that had disappeared the year before, a dog taken because of his breed for a Christmas gift. I realized this was a new category: stolen.

TAKEN NOT LOST

A dog named Benny was missing in Missouri, and his owners were distraught. He had wandered off their property, and I saw him visiting a dog friend. Then I saw him captured and locked up by a neighbor. I asked for spiritual interference to have him released so he could return home. Instead of bringing Benny back, they dropped him off in front of the Ace Hardware.

This was a rural area, and most people knew each other. Benny thought he could find his way home. I channeled him shortly after this, and he had gotten lost in a woodsy area, and then fell. While channeling him, I was afraid he was dead, the pain on his head and nose were so bad. He had fallen off a rock shelf area, and dropped many feet, lying crumpled at the base.

Several hunters found Benny, and were concerned that he would die without medical attention. The hunters took him back to camp, and then drove home with Benny. These people had several kids that immediately fell in love with him. After a few days, the kids couldn't bear the thought of Benny leaving the family. This was coupled with the fact that they lived several hours away (and hundreds of miles) from where they had found him.

What I realized several weeks into working with Benny was that he no longer was a "lost" dog as much as he was a "stolen" dog. Dogs taken by car somewhere are much less likely to find their way home; the effectiveness of their internal tracking device is greatly reduced by traveling long distances in vehicles.

The only dog client still missing up to the point when I started working with Benny was a Shar Pei, Sarah. Sarah had been walking her neighborhood, when a man in a black car snatched her. He had been looking for a Shar Pei to give his daughter as a Christmas gift. Shar Pei's were rare and expensive at the time so it was like stealing money.

I envisioned Sarah crossing over seven different bridges, not possible in many locations, but from New York City that was the exact number of bridges needed to cross to take the dog into New Jersey. The man gave Sarah as a Christmas present to his daughter.

I was shown the girl playing with Sarah in a room in a house that had a Christmas tree. Out of the thousands of people that live in New Jersey, I had no further knowledge of what house Sarah was in. With all the people in New York, and across the bridges to New Jersey, Sarah was hidden, the path not clear.

A third dog, a German shepherd named Chuck was stolen a few months after Benny. I was called because the owner thought Chuck was lost. When I looked into the situation, I saw Chuck run off, then up to some hunters who were camping out for an evening after a day of hunting. These hunters were impressed with Chuck, a gorgeous German shepherd who was well trained and lovingly behaved. In fact Chuck made such an impression on the hunters that when they left they took Chuck with them.

I couldn't understand why I was not finding these dogs. Then one day it struck me; they weren't lost dogs, they were stolen dogs. Dogs that could not get loose and find their way home. The dogs were living new lives, and being loved by new people.

HUNTER'S TALE

Some dogs have a past that their owners can only guess about. Telltale clues like flinching at a quick hand movement, or shaking in the presence of a man, reveal that they have a past that wasn't always kind. Some dogs, well, some dogs are lost, having been abandoned by the humans that provided them with safe harbor and promised to protect them.

At the Boulder City Art Festival in Nevada, I met a dog named Hunter. His owner said she had just adopted him and had no idea what his life was before her. So I asked him.

Hunter shared with me that he had been living with a family in Los Angeles. They had been enjoying a day at the park, when his owners drove away. Hunter was ashamed that he couldn't track them. He went on for several heartbreaking minutes talking about how he had a great nose and could follow most anything. However the reality was it was difficult to follow the scent of a car and he was afraid of traffic.

Hunter felt he was to blame for inadequate abilities. He apologized for not being able to track them. Hunter missed the little girl he belonged to and he cursed himself for not being a better tracker. He had let his family down. Then he was captured and brought to an animal control.

Dogs that are taken by car somewhere are much more likely to be unable to find their way home. The effectiveness of their internal tracking instinct is greatly reduced by traveling long distances in vehicles.

When a car gets involved, most dogs have a much harder time getting their bearings and finding their way home. I have talked to many lost dogs, which, not understanding that their owners had dumped them admitted that they were failures when it came to following their owner's home.

Hunter continued, telling me that he had been at a shelter several times before. Previous to the L.A. family, he lived in Reno and was left in a house that was foreclosed on. That became another time he found himself in a shelter. Hunter's life read like a novel, replete with tragedy, and abandonment along with hope for a better life. His current owner was his fourth home, and Hunter was on his best behavior so it could be his last one.

After talking to Hunter and sharing his story with his current owner, I felt the absurdity of what I was saying, thinking the owner was not going to be able to validate any of it. Many people still aren't sure if animal communicators are the real deal, even with specific details. I could be making the whole thing up. (If you are able to spend any length of time listening to me channel, you would realize that there is no way that I have the imagination to quickly invent the myriad of information that comes through me.)

Surprisingly, Hunter was from Best Friends Animal Sanctuary, and he was micro-chipped. Every time he had been abandoned, he went back to Best Friends, where a record of his experiences was kept; where he had lived and what had happened. His current owner could confirm that she was Hunter's fourth home and that a family had recently abandoned him in Los Angeles.

LOST CATS

"Nothing cuts me to the quick faster,
descends my heart to my shoes, and leaves me panic-stricken more than
a cat that does not come home one night.
Especially a cat that has consistently made it home
every night for many, many years.
With a lost cat, I blame myself,
which can very quickly turn to misery."
~ Ann Hoff

The reality is that I too, have had cats walk out of the house, never to return. So when someone calls with a lost cat, a part of me remembers I have had the same experience. I share this because the key to connecting with and finding an animal is to keep your fear and your ego out of it, and to remain neutral. My memories of having lost cats actually hinder me when looking for them. If I cannot push my emotions to the sidelines, I am of less use.

Luckily, as a Channeller, the information comes through me, not from me. However, the more I interact with clients and their missing animals, the more I am vested in the animal being found. There are a thousand reasons why a cat disappears; most of them have nothing to do with their human. When they find themselves lost, they need only make one bad turn and suddenly their lives are in jeopardy.

When people call me because they've lost cat, I have to tell them that cats approach death much differently from humans. The curtain between life and death is more transparent to cats, not opaque like it is for humans (as well as dogs). Cats can see into the next life and into the life before. For cats, dying is similar to walking from the living room into the kitchen; most have no fear of death (in fact many times they are more afraid of water!).

Most cats will not choose to suffer. Many cats also feel that dying is an extremely private ritual, which is why many of them go off by themselves to die. A lost cat often is a dying cat. However numerous cats on the other side have shared with me that they loved their humans so much they did not disappear, but decided to die with their humans present.

With lost cats rules are different from dogs. Many cats I talk to that are lost simply don't think they're lost. They're planning on coming back one day or are just doing a "walkabout." In some cases the feline will have found somebody else to give them energy, food, love and a place where they feel more suited. The cat will tell me whether or not they feel like they're lost. Knowing that the cat doesn't feel the same way as its owner (who is typically desperate to find them) at times leaves me in a quandary.

Many people will take in a found cat. It makes no difference if they are micro chipped or not; the cat may never get close enough to a microchip reader for it to do any good. Statistically 51% of household cats are strays. Collars usually aren't feasible because cats tend to hate them and they can get hung up on something, occasionally resulting in death. A breakaway collar could suffice instead. However if the collar breaks away, so does all the contact information attached to it.

Some cats come for a meal, or a day, and next year they may still be sitting beside you on the couch. This is an amazing gift cats have but can also be a downfall. I cannot tell you how many people call me looking for lost cats, only to find when I check in with the cats that they are not lost at all, but are hanging out with new people. Love your cats, knowing that they have chosen to be with you and that they know more about your trials and tribulations than you could ever imagine. Know that cats are by your side not in spite of, but because of your human condition.

DO YOU LET YOUR CAT OUT DOORS?

Statistics from the Humane Society say that outdoor cats live an average of two and a half years. Statistics are just an overall view, however, and individual results can sometimes be vastly different. I had the same cat family for seventeen years, BooBoo and Speedy. Although they went outside, they were primarily indoor cats.

Speedy loved to hunt, and lived to twenty-six. Booboo disappeared one night, taken by an owl I was told. The silence that fateful night told me that he was gone for good, leaving without saying goodbye. My current felines, Elvis and Spike, are usually in bed each night by ten.

The scariest time is when you first let cats out; they need to be able to find their way around and back to the house. Elvis slipped out on a hot summer afternoon once when I was taking my dog Patsy for a walk. After I returned, I was sitting down at the computer and I heard loud meowing at the door. Elvis swept in, panting hysterically, too hot, and afraid that he had been disconnected from his food source. Elvis has never wandered further from the house than the mailbox, though he loves to run up to the roof or on the top of the backyard brick fence.

OUTDOOR CATS

It only takes one open door, one pause in judgment, or perhaps a visitor who needs to keep the door open while packing in their suitcases. Some shelters will not adopt out cats unless the new owner promises never to let them outdoors.

While the American Humane Society makes it very clear that outdoor cats may lead lives of fear, facing calamities from automobile accidents to becoming lunch for larger predators, I have always successfully owned both indoor and outdoor cats. My cats are happy, mellow, and content, but are also exhilarated from running through tree branches, on top of the roof, chasing lizards, field mice, and gophers, as well as bagging the occasional pack rat.

According to Cat Kibble, 72% of household cats are indoors only. Of course, many of these are apartment cats that cannot fend for themselves outside with traffic, city life and multiple threats to their survival.

Rural cats face other threats: wild animals, getting lost, picking up illnesses from other cats. Most of the cats I talk to feel that being outside adds an additional dimension and joy to their lives. Remember, these are beings that do not fear death and thrive on investigating new spaces. Luckily, the place most cats like best is to be snuggled next to you.

PROTECTING YOUR CATS

I like to let cats out of the house for a few minutes when I can watch them, so they can acclimate to the surroundings. Many of the lost cats I have looked for were indoor cats. Indoor cats usually aren't micro-chipped and are often de-clawed which leaves them vulnerable.

PEARL

I worked with Susan for over ten years in my medical sales career. She had given me Speedy (my cat that lived into his mid-twenties) as a kitten.

Sue called me in distress; her cat Pearl was missing. Her husband came home from a business trip late at night. When he was carrying in his luggage, Pearl ran out the door. Sue looked everywhere for Pearl, to no avail. So she called me.

When I started channeling Pearl, the first information that came through was that she was still alive. Then Pearl shared that when she got outside, something chased her almost immediately, so she fled. She sent me a picture telepathically; her pursuer was a dark shadow, the size of a coyote.

Pearl turned left, ran straight for a few blocks, then swerved off the road she was on and ran up a tree.

Looking at a map of the area, I was shocked to find that Susan's house was adjacent to a National Forest and several canyons. Pearl was up a tree in a thick dark wilderness.

Pearl shared the view from her perch, along with the landmarks she saw. In cases like this, I don't know why I get land markers such as a red roof and a tall pine, instead of an address or a geographical location. With all the power that the spirit guides and angels have, it seems that they could find a way to be more precise. Up a tree in a forest is not necessarily the best way to specify a location.

Sue and I looked for days for Pearl, not knowing how to isolate her location. Unfortunately, we weren't successful finding Pearl, but Sue was able to receive closure by talking to Pearl again, realizing and processing her tremendous guilt about Pearl getting outside. In the end, Pearl felt it was easier to come back in a new body than to try to find her way out of the woods.

GILES

Spike's brother Giles (I called him the Cary Grant of cats because he was so handsome) was a brown tabby with white paws and a white bib. Giles just loved attention, and he loved to visit other homes. I put Giles on a leash and walked him with the dogs. Giles was Spike's full sibling from the farm. I took Spike with me back to Tucson one August and then, over the Christmas holidays, brought Giles back to Tucson too. In those few extra months on the farm, Giles became ill with a chronic respiratory infection. My Tucson vet recommended that Giles get healthier before he was neutered, and he gave me antibiotics for him. Knowing Giles's wanderlust, I put a collar on him with my contact information.

After I left for work, Giles would stride off down the road. This had nothing to do with food and everything to do with him getting human attention. In one week, I had to get Giles three times, once six miles from my house. With the exercise of the walk, Giles used parts of his lungs that he hadn't been using before and coughed up green sputum. The panicked calls I got from people weren't about having found Giles as much as they were about fear of catching whatever it was that Giles had in his lungs.

It took six months to get Giles completely healthy; then he was neutered. Giles went from being on the road constantly to lounging around the house, not even going outside. His collar broke and I didn't think to replace it. So when he disappeared for four days, I made the mental note that I needed to keep Giles locked in when he came back again. Then the Christmas holidays came, and I went back to Illinois for a week. During my absence, Giles made one last appearance, but my house sitter didn't lock him inside the house as I had requested.

About two months later, I received a panic-stricken psychic phone call from Giles. He was about to get declawed and wanted help to stop it. His new family kept him locked up, and he couldn't get back to me. Giles had made his choice; and it imprisoned him.

ALEX AND IKO

Alex called me, hysterical from having lost her cat IKO. The previous week Iko had all of her teeth pulled because of severe decay. She had been declawed years earlier. Iko was totally defenseless and didn't know his way around the neighborhood. Unfortunately, I saw her met an untimely death and she was never heard from again.

Iko's story illuminates one of the many reasons I do not condone declawing cats. Cats can be taught to be respectful and to only use their claws on a scratching post. My current cats, Elvis and Spike never use their claws on the furniture or me. Spike won't even use his claws on the dogs, and Elvis bites before scratching someone.

A cat without claws in the outside world is extremely vulnerable. Most cat owners say: "Oh, well, the cat never gets out." But it only takes once, and I can't tell you how many people call me that their lost cat got out "just this once." Then the de-clawed cat is out of the home, alone and without protection. Typically, these owners feel extremely guilty, because there's not much else that they can do at this point.

TIPS ON LOOKING FOR LOST PETS

Every hour, the ability to find and track lost pets becomes better. There are now dogs that track smell that can see where a pet has gone, people like myself, equipment like Tagg and GPS systems that are getting smaller. However, I have a suspicion that pets will keep getting lost. I cannot tell you how many people who have "house" cats had them just get out once- with dire consequences. The best we can do is get better at finding them, and make sure that no loved one gets killed needlessly in a shelter as a stray.

Suggestions if your pet goes missing:

1. TIME IS OF THE ESSENCE. Don't wait for the animal to come back. Better be overprotective than careless. Act fast.

2. Call an animal intuitive within the first 48 hours. An Intuitive's ability to find an animal and give you useful data is much cleaner if the trail is still warm. While you may feel that you should also have the "intuitive connection" (believe me, you do), it is almost impossible to put fear out of your head and be neutral enough to be accurate.

3. Ask your pet's spirit guides to protect them. Then go for special teams. St. Anthony, St. Francis, Archangel Michael, Archangel Raphael and Ganesha are the beings I use. Call on and work with whomever you believe in. If you don't believe in spiritual beings try this anyway. Suspend belief. It costs nothing. Surround your pet with light, love and protection.

4. Make "lost pet" signs using your pet's photo. State any identifying marks or habits. Put signs up in your neighborhood and in post offices, libraries, pet supply stores, veterinary offices, feed stores and grocery stores. Think of a common area where people congregate. If your pet responds to their name, add that fact. Add phone numbers so that the rescuer can contact you regardless of the time of day. (I had two dogs show up at my house once, only to have their company the entire day, because the owners had not included their work number on the dogs' tags.)

5. Realize that other people may know what has happened to your pet, especially if someone has taken your dog to be their dog. I have seen the pressure from posted fliers and pleadings cause searched for pets to suddenly appear at a shopping mall, or to be spotted at a location across town. Making the new "owners" feel guilty and remorseful is the best way to have the pet returned.

6. Go to the last place your pet was seen, both physically and

mentally. Envision the path they took, and see the logical place they would go. Search your neighborhood; ask everyone; offer a reward. By utilizing and implementing this comprehensive spiritual and pragmatic approach, more people will become involved. I had a client that lost their dog on the beach while visiting Mexico. No one on the beach could find the dog. My client offered a reward, and the dog miraculously appeared two hours later.

7. Call your pet's name and check any places they could have become trapped, such as in garages or under vehicles. A lost pet often hides during the day, so be sure to go out again at night with a flashlight and call for them. Bring a can of food to lure a hungry and scared pet to you.

8. Register with the local shelters and animal control agencies. As a puppy, Patsy escaped one afternoon. I called the Humane Society and the County Rescue. I checked if she was in the Rescue, and by the time I got back, the Humane Society called stating that a woman found Patsy trying to cross a street, then took her home to make sure she didn't get run over. Patsy was lost for three dreadful hours. Long enough for her rescuer to snap 60 pictures of her while she posed on the bed.

9. Call the company that has the microchip data. Check your groomer and veterinarian- brainstorm for solutions. Remember to network with everyone and leave your flyers.

10. Place ads in local newspapers and magazines. If someone has found your pet this will help him or her do the right thing. (Offer a reward in case someone found your untagged pet and was thinking of keeping him).

11. Utilize other modes of communication. Many radio and TV stations broadcast free lost pet information. Internet sites like petfinder.com are a must. LookingforToto.com will call all houses in your area. New sites are appearing every day, so do a comprehensive search.

12. Read the found ads. Respond to any that could be close to your pet's description. Keep in mind that a week of wandering the

streets can make white pets drab gray, and healthy pets gaunt and thin. The ad's description might not exactly fit.

13. If I could give you anything, it would be the knowledge that you and your pet are connected still, even when you are physically apart. Remember, nothing is lost in God's world.

BEHAVIOR
ISSUES

*"I have talked to quite a few people about
the bad things their animals do.
Along the way I have discovered that bad behavior in animals can
often be traced back to something a human did or did not do.
If you want to resolve a problem, start by figuring out what created it."
~ Marta Williams, Ask Your Animals*

The majority of clients I work with have behavior issues with their pets. That is why this section is the largest. What follows is a wide array of behavior problems that have come my way, most of which I have had the opportunity to clear and heal. I always give the animal itself the opportunity to talk about the issues, and honor them by hearing their truth.

The reason things are happening can be widely varied. When my practice was in its infancy, I placed an ad in a Tucson paper saying I cured 100% of "peeing issues". I charged clients for the first session and then followed up with subsequent sessions if the problem didn't disappear or reappeared. What I found, was that the second time I was called in to talk to the pet, it was always a different reason than the one I previously had talked to them about. I found this fascinating. I am sharing the stories of clients that I have found memorable, Interactions that helped me to comprehend the human animal bond at a much different level. There is always more to the story then what is instantly seen, and until you find out the details from the animals firsthand, the whole story is not visible.

WHO YOU GONNA CALL?

If you compare what I do to training experts, the information and techniques actually dovetail very nicely. First of all, with animal communication, you're able to get the point of view from your pets. You can compare it to sitting down for negotiations instead of manhandling your point of view as the right one. Perhaps many wars would have been avoided if we had taken the time for that. I have seen many dogs change their behavior immediately, because their humans respected them enough to listen.

Bad behavior may actually be caused by the pet not getting something they want or need, and so they are protesting the only way they can: acting out, or defecating somewhere they shouldn't. If instead of valuing your pet's feelings, you come down hard on them for bad behavior, ruling with an iron fist, it will leave them confused and distrustful. Instead of a partnership, you will have a dictatorship. The alpha dog training without communication can be a dictatorship, bear in mind that this is the animal's whole life.

Most dog trainers *are* dog trainers because they love animals. People go to school for almost two decades learning to be good citizens; pets can benefit from education as well. I often find both cats and dogs watching TV to learn. And I know that if you provide additional training for your pet, they will be learning sponges, and you both will enjoy your new relationships.

EVA AND REX

"I believe all animals are sentient.
Each species has its own priorities and physical abilities that
affect how its intelligence is displayed.
But the notion that animals are not as smart as humans are incorrect:
their intelligence is just different than ours.
When you start communicating intuitively with animals,
you will begin to perceive the unique intelligence of each
species and each individual."
~ Marta Williams, Ask Your Animals

One Sunday, I found myself at a bustling Unity Church open house in Tucson, AZ. Although it had seemingly started out as a normal Sunday, it quickly changed into a very abnormal day—one that ultimately led me to make a career change and divert my life path permanently. As I walked into the church, I saw several crowded rooms. In the midst of them was a stressed woman in a wheelchair talking to the equally stressed golden retriever by her side.

The dog looked around uneasily, without making eye contact, and was hesitant to sit down. He shifted his weight from paw to paw, another sign that he was uncomfortable. I approached the woman, who introduced herself as Eva.

"I happen to be an animal communicator; may I talk to your dog?"

Eva graciously agreed. "Yes, please do. His name is Rex. He is in training to be my new service dog, but he doesn't seem to want to do what I need today. I try to get him to do good at the service dog lessons, but he hardly ever does. I've told him that if he doesn't do better next week, I may have to get a different service dog."

I focused on Rex, and immediately received a picture of pointed cowboy boots, kicking him. I also could feel what it had felt like, being kicked viciously, without warning. It *was* painful and confusing for Rex. He couldn't figure out what to do to stop the abuse, but he knew that cowboy boots represented pain. I felt a shiver as I tuned in deeper to Rex and created a stage in my mind to receive additional information.

Rex told me he looks at the feet of every person coming in to see if they are wearing cowboy boots. With that kind of stress, he doesn't have much energy left to pay attention to Eva.

I felt the presence of another dog, a chocolate lab, and the name Buddy came through. Then I experienced a deep feeling of sadness that almost caused me to start crying.

"Who is Buddy?" I asked Eva.

"Oh, Buddy!" Eva exclaimed, and then started crying out loud so frantically it could be described as bawling. Tears streamed down her face. "He was my last dog. He was such a good service dog I really enjoyed him. In fact, I ask him to come down from heaven and help Rex learn how to do this service dog stuff."

"May I ask you a question about Buddy?"

"Of course," Eva said.

"Was buddy cremated?"

"Yes."

"Do you still have the ashes?"

"Yes, I got a cardboard box with the ashes. I didn't want to throw them away, so he is in my bedroom closet."

Keeping the ashes was having an impact on Rex. I have found that when a human keeps the ashes of their pets, the spirit usually remains (a situation that is called earthbound). Keeping the ashes seems to indicate to the spirits of deceased pets that they are still needed here. Dogs come to earth with a purpose, and they don't want to give up that purpose even when they're no longer in possession of their physical bodies.

I explained this to Eva. "I know keeping Buddy's ashes may seem like a good way to honor him, and you didn't understand the implications. So don't feel like you've done something wrong. A lot of people keep ashes of their dogs. The animals make their own choice to go to the light or stay here on earth. You didn't know. But," I assured her; "I can send Buddy to heaven if you give me permission."

I was feeling how attached she was to keeping Buddy with her. "I know it feels great to have Buddy around, but if he stays earthbound, for him, it is the same as when he was alive, just without his body. Everything he had before, his pain, his fear, is still with him. He goes to heaven, he will be able to be with you at the speed of thought, and he will be in a space of blissful joy. He can also reincarnate and come back to you in a different body. We can talk to Buddy and see how he feels about coming back, but we need to send him to heaven now."

"As far as Rex," I continued, "He is seeing and feeling Buddy. Pets are much more sensitive to the spirit world than humans. They can see earthbound spirits, hear and feel their presence. I have countless clients who have confirmed that their pets are interacting with earthbound energy."

I switched to the other issue at hand, "When you ask Buddy to help Rex, what exactly are you saying?

"I am telling Rex, you *have* to learn. Buddy, bless his soul did this so well. Buddy if you are anywhere around here, help Rex to get through the training and learn the program easier!"

"That jives with what I was shown. Rex is afraid that Buddy is going to come back and take his job, and then Rex would leave. He is very insecure, and you threaten him daily. I need you to make the commitment to Rex and believe in him a little bit. Can you look me in the eye and say that you will believe in Rex and help him through the training? He is a young dog, who has this abuse issue. I can clear his energy which will give Rex the ability to focus. As Rex gets older, he will get smarter and your bond will get stronger."

After Eva gave me permission, I cleared Rex's energy and put love and protection around him (see Appendix's five and six).

The next day an animal psychic from Phoenix messaged me: "I don't know what you did, but the animals thank you. They thank you a lot. Your work with the animals will raise the vibration of the world."

I followed up with Eva six months later. Buddy was in heaven. Rex was doing great after his energy clearing. He was a fantastic service dog who loved his purpose and knew he had a forever home.

THE KATRINA DOG: DEALING WITH LICKING

Terry was a rescue that came from New Orleans after Katrina. Her new owner, Diane, called me because Terry was licking people incessantly; she just couldn't sit next to a person and be still. She was constantly licking her owner and everyone else on their hands or their knee. When I asked the spirit guides what had happened to Terry to cause such behavior, they showed me Terry with an older woman. Even though Terry licked her continuously, the woman failed to respond. This was because the lady had suffered a fatal heart attack. With all the upheaval and confusion during and after Hurricane Katrina, no one came by and noticed that this had happened for several days. Terry was left alone with her deceased owner, unable to do anything to change the situation. Now she needed constant reminders that the people in her life were okay and unharmed.

Many pets have nervous habits that get out of control. Just like people, they can self-mutilate or exhibit obsessive-compulsive behaviors. I experience it as a thought loop that goes through a pet's mind like, "I have an itch, I have an itch." Sometimes it starts with an actual itch, and then turns into a behavioral habit that becomes harmful.

I typically find out the cause of the dog's behavior asking their story. Sometimes, all it takes is just talking to the pet to get them to quit the behavior. Often, breaking the ability to lick or scratch themselves by putting a shirt or socks on the affected area goes a long way. Another culprit can be allergies causing the dogs to lick and scratch themselves, and usually a doggie dose of Benadryl or a cortisone allergy pack does wonders if that is the correct diagnosis.

When I was in pharmaceuticals, I sold antidepressants to physicians to prescribe for humans. Depression is actually easy to treat compared to OCD (obsessive compulsive disorder) in humans. If the pet doesn't have allergies or a thought link that can be broken by clearing energy, then pharmaceutical treatment for OCD can be helpful. Treatment with Serotonin reuptake inhibitors (Prozac, Paxil, Zoloft) will reduce the frequency of the obsessive behavior such as scratching and licking.

With pets that suffer from OCD, it has been my experience that they respond successfully to treatment. One thing to be aware of is that in humans, Prozac never received the indication for OCD, but Paxil did. Many veterinarians just think of Prozac when they think of an SSRI (selective serotonin reuptake inhibitor). With humans, Paxil is thought of as more calming, while Prozac is thought of as more activating. So if you have a hyperactive dog that is tearing apart everything including his hide, Paxil is the better choice. However, neither one of these drugs has an indication for dogs; so consult your veterinarian before using.

With Terry, clearing the energy of the memory of her previous owners death allowed her to trust life again. The licking slowed down, and then new healthy behaviors like walks took her mind off of constantly checking on her human's health.

DEALING WITH EXCREMENT

Of the all behavior issues I am brought in on, peeing and defecating are the most common. The reasons for these behaviors are numerous. But instead of treating all pets the same you can uncover the source of the behavior. Communicating with your pets and finding out the reason for such behaviors means you are treating them with respect.

If there's an earthbound spirit around, pets will try to protect their owners. This can manifest as the pet peeing around the human's bed, chair or room boundaries.

A change in martial status can also be the cause of these behaviors, as can a change in less committed relationships. Dogs with a purpose of guarding you will stay around your bed to make sure that an ex-lover doesn't come back. If you think the way a dog does, it makes perfect sense; there is spirit energy in the room and they pee boundary lines around your space to protect you.

There are two reasons why this happens; one is a result of alpha dog behavior, and the other is that some dogs simply can't handle strong emotions. Consider the alpha dog; protecting those in the pack that are weaker, which manifests as peeing (marking territory) around the weaker member (if you are the one in bed and crying, that makes you weaker). Second, dogs are intricately connected to us intuitively and physically. Some simply cannot handle the intensity of the situation when humans cry. Humans and dolphins are the only two species that cry tears. What I have found is dogs will howl or pee in empathy. I have seen many cases of this behavior.

Think about it this way. Dogs live in a *family*. When your mother cries, doesn't that make you cry sometimes? Every time I split with a boyfriend that my heart broke I would lie on the couch crying, my dog Mandy howling right alongside me. Often, defecating on the rug next to the couch followed up the howling.

When Mandy did this, however, I felt that she wasn't on my team—that she was acting out because a boyfriend was gone (at this time, I hadn't yet realized I was able to talk to the animals). It took several bouts of boyfriends leaving before I realized that Mandy was defecating and peeing because she couldn't handle the intensity of the situation.

Horses in the wild mark their territory with excrement and urine, so that when a new stallion comes into the territory, he knows who the land belongs to.

HOME DEPOT DOG

The Stewarts had a gorgeous Papillion named Barry. When I first met Mr. Stewart at Home Depot, a picture of Barry was the only one in his wallet. Barry had several instances of "mistakes" and I was called in more than once to correct his behavior. The first time, it was habitual bad behavior; Barry mistakenly thought it was okay to pee in the house. The energy associated with that behavior was cleared, and Barry transitioned to using the yard or waited until taken for a walk. I explained the "pee-stick" process (see Appendix).

The Stewarts contacted me a second time for Barry's inappropriate urination. Mrs. Stewart had an ex-husband who'd passed away (she was unaware of this at the time; she had to make some calls to confirm the situation). Deciding to stay earthbound, the man was trying to reunite with her after death. Barney could see him, and urinated around Mrs. Stewart's chair to protect her.

A final session occurred with Barry a few months later. He began having accidents again, this time on the carpet. When I questioned him, he brought up that Mr. Stewart stayed up late at night and would snack on ice cream, chips, chocolate and plenty of stuff that a dog should never eat. He shared these treats with Barry, but Barry was too polite to say it was making him sick. The accidents came from an upset digestive tract, and once the midnight treats stopped, so did the deposits on the carpet.

THE CONTRACT KILLER AND THE BICHONS

'I've seen a look in dogs' eyes,
a quickly vanishing look of amazed contempt, and
I am convinced that dogs think humans are nuts."
~ John Steinbeck

Sandy contacted me about her Bichon Frise dogs that were peeing in the house. When I entered her Tucson foothills home, I immediately knew an earthbound spirit was present. Her male dog was peeing around the perimeter of the living room to protect the space for the family. I contacted the spirit. He shared that he had been a hit man for the mob, murdered numerous people, and still attended a Catholic church every Sunday.

At death, the hit man had vaguely remembered stories of going to heaven, being judged and sent down to hell. He realized if anyone deserved to be punished, he did. So when he died, he decided to stay earthbound and attached to the house he died in. Then Sandy's family moved in, and the hit man attached to them. Ted and Sally, Sandy's Bichons, were protecting the family from his fairly sinister energy.

I cleared the hit man from the house and sent him to heaven. Sandy had the carpets cleaned, and Ted and Sally's peeing issue was solved.

An important thing to keep in mind, however, is that after energy is cleared like this, the belief system of the human involved also needs to be changed. Sandy raged at her dogs: "You're going to pee on the carpets again, right after I pay five hundred dollars for cleaning the rugs!" The dogs did not meet her eyes, and scurried under the table when she yelled. I had to remind her that things were different now and not to start punishing the dogs for something they had not yet done. That would recreate the situation again, unless she too, dropped the memory and moved to neutral.

MR WIZARD'S DRAMA

My husband and I are either going to buy a dog or have a child.
We can't decide whether to ruin our carpets or ruin our lives."
~ *Rita Rudner*

"The first year I was in practice as an intuitive, Nicky called me because her Yorkshire terrier, Mr. Wizard, was peeing in the house.

Nicky had recently separated from her husband, and her daughter, Jody, still lived with her. Nicky and her husband owned a business together in a local mall so she saw him there everyday. For some reason, he still came in the house, and used the phone in the bedroom to check his messages. The bedroom phone was the only one in the house. This was after the millennium, yet surprisingly; no one in this family had a cell phone.

Mr. Wizard was very alarmed with the intrusion of male energy into the bedroom. He had listened as the couple fought about possible divorce, and was sure he heard that the man of the house had been kicked out and was *gone*. With dogs, if you say to someone, "I never want to see you again," they take it as the gospel truth. This causes the canine to be really surprised when the spouse shows up again. Dogs don't lie, and they don't think that anyone else will lie either. They take what you say to heart, whether it is to them or between other members of the family.

Mr. Wizard was peeing around the house marking his territory from the absent husband. He wasn't having very good luck at it since the man was still coming into the bedroom. I told my client to establish some guidelines and boundaries.

Nicky was of German descent, and her husband's family came from the Middle East. Neither of them was born in the United States. The separated husband was raised with the idea that you didn't get divorced. He hired a contractor with a felony murder conviction to repair the roof and then was out of town when the payment was due. Perhaps if the money were not paid, the contractor would get physical (needless to say, this household was full of high-adrenaline drama).

Instead, the contractor offered a shoulder for Nicky to cry on and they became close. I never discovered how far this progressed, but Nicky felt guilty because of the liaison. After all, he was a convicted felon but he genuinely cared for her. Nicky was distraught, dealing with major shifts in her life. She did not have anyone to talk to or guide her.

The couple continued to work together, acting civil. She worked so much that she didn't have any friends outside work. Nikki actually told me that she felt that if she had not had her daughter, she would have committed suicide. She had made a commitment to her daughter. Her plan was to raise her daughter to eighteen, then kill herself. She had no plans after that.

When we were alone, Nikki's daughter, Jody, lifted up her skirt and showed me parallel lines on her leg that looked like open scratches (kind a cat might make) but they were executed with more precision and longer than cat scratches. Jody told me she was cutting herself. Her parents didn't know, but it was the only thing she found to help relieve the pressure. Then she told me to please not tell her mom.

Mr. Wizard was living with an incredible amount of emotional turmoil. In several sessions he was barely mentioned, while Nikki ranted on about the marital problems. If I focused on the dog behavior, the human issues always came up along with them.

A person's story needs to be told. When the words hit air, they are seen more clearly, and new solutions appear. The issues do not seem as tawdry and hopeless. The angels and guides get a chance to intervene.

After I cleared the energy and set strict boundaries on the home, Mr. Wizard quit peeing in the house.

I got called in once more, when Mr. Wizard had a relapse. It had been raining and instead of going out he peed inside. When I spoke to him, he immediately said he didn't like getting his paws wet or coming back in with wet feet. The solution was a towel placed by the door so Mr. Wizard could wipe his paws. Once again he became the perfect canine companion.

This is an example of why communication is needed. Mr. Wizard's relapse was totally unrelated to the first peeing episodes. Don't automatically assume that a repeated behavior issue is about the same source. What's happening can be something totally new. And you need to look at each situation separately.

GLENDA

Men had always ordered my client Glenda around, treating her like a second-class citizen. Currently she was dating a man who was mean to her, and though she thought she was standing up to him, she really wasn't. He had given Glenda a ring, which she wanted to give back but "he wouldn't take it." While I was talking about this mess with her, her dog, Duchess whined and placed a paw on my leg. I felt Duchess's concern.

When I shared this information, Glenda snapped back: "What difference does it make to her? Her life isn't going to change either way."

That answer astounded me. Duchess's life would change completely if the boyfriend were gone. It would be less stressful, more organized, and calmer. With the boyfriend present, Duchess marinated daily in a high-octane atmosphere of discord, anger and tension. If environmental factors were not addressed, there was a high probability of future behavioral problems.

A PHONE CLIENT WITH PEEING ISSUES: AND A SOLUTION

In a separate case a client had a dog that was peeing around the house while she slept. I told her that was easy enough; she could put the dog in a crate a night. She said that when she crated the dog, he howled all night and she couldn't get any rest. I asked if she could move the crate, and she told me that wasn't an option.

This dog was protective peeing, but the woman didn't want to address the situation. I cleared the energy on both the house and the dog.

At that time, I asked the spirit guides for a physical solution about what to do for a dog peeing at night without putting them in a cage. Later that evening, I was switching channels and came across Letterman. I usually don't watch him, but stopped for a moment to see who was on the show. It happened to be Jane Lynch who plays Sue Sylvester on Glee. Suddenly, Jane was talking about her dog, and showed Dave a picture of her dog with diapers on! She said the dog didn't know any better, she just thought that was how she should routinely be dressed. The spirit guides tapped me on the shoulder. This was the answer to the question of what to do with the dog that wouldn't be quiet in the crate.

PEEING AND POOPING ISSUES WITH CATS

Some cats will pee outside the litter box because they don't like stirring up the dust that comes from digging in the clay litter. They may also poop outside the box because they are upset at you. I even had a client's whose cat was not using the litter box because she wasn't allowed to do her purpose (the reason she came to be with her human).

Spike, my cat, has pooped outside the box on several specific occasions.

I was working on my kitchen, when I felt two taps on my shoulder, just as a person would do to have you turn around. I whirled swinging hard, expecting an intruder. I realized a moment too late that it was Spike, sitting on the counter. I was unable to stop my blow. He fled visibly upset. I didn't see him again till late the next day. In protest, he defecated three inches outside his litter box for the next five days.

Another instance of Spike's rebellion occurred when I disagreed with him about what to do with a mouse that was in the living room. I have detested mice since the days my brother, fresh from grinding corn had a mouse up his pants leg. He grabbed the mouse by the tail and chased me around the house with it.

I was raised that mice should be for cat food, not pets. My dog Patsy chased the mouse to my living room, into a cranny in the fireplace wall. I wanted to make sure it was caught, so I brought Spike to the crack hoping he would like his ancestors, those cats of my childhood, pick up a scent and camp out until the mouse reappeared. But Spike just walked away, indifferent.

I was insistent on getting the mouse, so I took a leash and tied Spike in front of the space, in retrospect, not my finest moments. Spike sat with his back to the opening until I released him several hours later. Defiantly, Spike pooped in front of his litter box for the next week.

CARMEL

Waiting for a doctor's appointment, Eileen thumbed through a cat magazine and found my ad. She had cat problems, and was quickly running out of options. She took it as the non-coincidence it was, and called me.

Eileen was living on the third floor of a Victorian house in San Francisco with over 20 cats and a newly adopted kitten. The kitten, Carmel, was not fitting in very well.

Two of the older cats had decided they didn't like Carmel, and like bullies on a schoolyard, would beat her up every chance they got. Terrorized so badly by the pair, when they just started moving towards Carmel, she would panic and defecate. When Eileen came home she would find Carmel sitting in her own excrement. Carmel was literally scared shitless.

After talking to the cats, I found that they resented Carmel, and they thought the apartment was crowded enough before she came. They wouldn't promise to quit bullying. In any case, Carmel reached the point where she needed some TLC (tender loving care). She had been taken from her mother a too soon and was not adept in taking care of herself and keeping her fur clean. To add to matters, Carmel had allergies that made her have spots where she scratched herself raw.

We decided that the best solution was to allow Carmel to live in Eileen's bedroom, so she could have her space and become more confident. We extracted a promise that Carmel would always use the litter box in the bedroom. This solution worked, and Eileen grew to love Carmel even more because of the close proximity in her life.

Carmel died two years later from an illness. She has since returned to Eileen, in a better body with longer legs, no allergies and deep friendships with the older cats.

LYNN AND DAVID

When I first met Lynn, her male cat, David, had been peeing on her boyfriend's clothes. This progressed to peeing on her boyfriend. After talking to them both, it was obvious David was looking out for his owner. The man was not a nice man, and the cat was protecting Lynn by peeing on him. After this discussion, Lynn decided that the best thing to do was to leave the boyfriend and live alone.

I sanctified the new place, and cleared energy on David. Thru telepathic communication I got across to David that he was safe, allowing him to feel unthreatened. That enabled him to quit peeing in the house. Lynn then gained enough strength to leave the man completely and move to another city. In a rather curious turn of events, however, the man had a major stroke just a few weeks after Lynn left, and he was admitted to the VA hospital indefinitely.

Several months later, Lynn called again. David had gone back to his old ways. Once again, he was peeing without using the litter box.

It was while working with these two that I had an epiphany. I could not control the way an animal acts after I talk to them anymore than I could a person's behavior.

Up to this point, I'd had an immaculate record. Every client's animal had resolved their negative behavior issues and had been able to change their actions. I now realized it had nothing to do with my so-called "talent" as it did the pets wanting to please their humans. Animals like a smooth running relationship.

Lynn had moved into a first floor apartment. The tenants in the adjoining upstairs apartment routinely drank and became incapacitated. The problem with this situation is that people who drink can attract negative energy, along with energy vampires. The exact words that the spirit guides use to describe it are as follows; "beings of low moral fortitude can be possessed by energy vampires."

David felt Lynn's anxiety-ridden angst. His spraying was his response, trying to stabilize the situation by marking the house that he was guarding. For the cat, it was an insurance policy, like lighting flares around your broken down vehicle at night. Lynn and I worked together to sanctify her space on a daily basis, and to use the exact protection prayer, adding essential oils and crystals to strength the clarity and power of the energy. One thing to always keep in mind when faced with a situation like Lynn's is that a spirit WITH a body (in other words someone who is alive) always has more power than someone without a body (for example a ghost, or a disconnected energy).

SCOUT AND THE CONFEDERATE COWBOYS
SPIRITUAL INTERFERENCE

Tracey called me to work with her German Shepherd, Scout, because he was peeing inside the house. She had seen my ad in the local paper that said I could stop inappropriate urination.

Tracey described Scout as a great dog, very loving and obedient. She explained that suddenly, a month earlier, he quit going outside to pee. Scout was seven and he had a history of being very regimented. Peeing on the throw rug inside the house was outside of his character.

Scout told me about four young cowboy energies. There were seven houses on the street that Tracey and Scout lived on. Their house backed up against the Tanque Verde Wash, in Tucson, where rivers don't run all year. Rather, Tucson has a system of dry washes. These are riverbeds that only have water in them a few times per year (In the 1800's, many of the wash beds had water in them all the time, and Tucson was far greener).

Earthbound, the cowboys cruised the houses that sat on the wash, acquiring energy. Tracey's house had been off limits because Scout would not let them in. The cowboys retaliated by waiting until Scout came outside, then they blocked the doggie door, not letting him back into the house. Scout decided to remedy the situation by not going outside at all if Tracey wasn't home. This was the reason he was peeing inside.

Whenever I talk to an earthbound energy, I honor it by finding out the reason they remain on this plane. These four earthbound cowboys told me their story.

They were confederate soldiers in the Civil War. When they realized that the south was losing, they headed west, hoping to avoid the worst of the fighting and to hide out until the war was over.

Almost defeated, the Confederates weren't pursuing deserters anymore.

However, all horses were considered to be property of the military. These men had joined the confederate army with their personal horses. One of the deserter's mounts was a loudly colored paint horse (think of Little Joe's horse in Bonanza). Prized steeds all, a wire was sent that these horses had been stolen.

The Tucson Sheriff spotted the Paint horse and the two others tied up downtown and tried to confiscate them. The cowboys galloped away, only to be captured at the edge of town and hung for thievery.

The sheriff got the gorgeous horse. Not prepared to be dead, the cowboys stayed earthbound. In their early twenties, they somehow expected they could go back to their wives; instead they were tethered to the spot where they had died and had been there ever since (there are really specific rules to being earthbound, but I do not know what they all consist of).

I sent the cowboys to heaven, and then cleared the energy in and around Tracey's house. Scout's energy was cleared, and a new intent was set in the space. Scout immediately went outside and started flirting with the neighbor's female dog by bouncing straight up to look over the fence. Scout remarked that he "looked dapper" with his blue bandana on.

Scout shared that his purpose was to protect Tracey, no matter what the cost. Then Tracey's father on the other side came thru, remarking that he had handpicked Scout (a dog that he knew could protect Tracey) from heaven.

I had been called to interact with Scout, and then Scout became the gateway for messages from the other side. Tracey's father loved her deeply, wanting her to know that he was still involved in her life. He shared seeing some of the recent activities in her life: a new pet bird, a job promotion and fall flowers being planted.

I thought the story would end there. However, I received a call from Tracey several weeks later. She told me that all the houses on the block were experiencing the same thing: their outside lights would not go on at night. When Tracey told me this, the first thing I thought was that I erred when sending the cowboy spirits to heaven. So we made another appointment.

Most of the time when I channel, I tape the session, so that I am not holding on to energy and stories that are not mine. There simply is not enough room in my head to keep all the information.

When I work with earthbound energies, I call their name; that is how I specify them. So I thought I got a name wrong and was going to have to adjust for that. However, when I started the new session with Scout and Tracey, a cowboy again came through and stated his name. Fortunately, Tracey had had the foresight to listen to the tape of the last session and immediately told me that this cowboy's name was a new one, not the name of someone from the previous session. I asked for the new spirit to be escorted to the other side.

In the end, I cleared 26 spirits from Tracey's house. Apparently, where her house was located had once served as the main road out of Tucson. Many deaths had occurred there, many stayed earthbound. Every spirit had a story to tell, of leaving or staying in Tucson. It was becoming ever more apparent to me that all earthbound spirits had a story, and that dogs could be witness to them.

EARTHBOUND ENERGIES

I get information from my spirit guides if a situation is caused by earthbound interference (more commonly known as ghosts). They can be an animal, like a dog or cat, or a person. I used to hesitate to discuss the energy interference because it meant I was one of the woo-woo crowd. Someone who talked to the dead and believed in ghosts.

What I discovered during these phone sessions is that 90 percent of the people that have an earthbound spirit present in their lives *knows* it is there. They know because the phone rings every morning at nine, or the dog barks in the corner of the kitchen every night at ten, or looks up at the ceiling incessantly when it seems nothing is there.

Cats and dogs both can see spiritual etheric beings, often interacting with them and trying to protect their humans from them. Earthbound spirits are not the same as someone who has "crossed over." They remain like the person they were when they were alive, only now they don't have a body.

In Temple Grandin's book, *Animals Make Us Human*, she mentions one of the family dogs going to a window, looking at another house and barking. She had no idea why that was happening. Reading this, I got a hit that there was a ghost in that other house. That's what the dog was barking at. The reason for this behavior is something a dog trainer many not notice. When I am called in, I can disperse the energy so that the dog is no longer freaked out by whatever is in the corner, or in the house next door.

Another example of this came from a client of mine that had a dog that suddenly started barking in the living room every night. When I looked at the situation, I saw an ex-husband who had recently died, who was coming back to be around my client. Although she was now married to another man, the ex-husband wanted a second chance. He didn't want to transition to heaven until he made his peace with her.

Some earthbound spirits have been on this plane for a long time. I once did a session in a brand new house containing the spirit of an American Indian woman. She had been killed during a skirmish between tribes. She had been looking for her son to make sure he was safe: for the last two hundred years. She heard me speaking and came into the room to see if I could help her. She was quite happy when she found I could send her on to heaven and that her son was already there.

The earthbound state is a limbo state. The spirit has no body, no energy of its own, and will attach to a person or a place. If it is manifesting (opening doors, flicking lights, interacting with pets) it is getting the energy from somewhere. This energy can come from the house (lights, a computer, or the phone) or another human.

Many times people who have autoimmune diseases (chronic fatigue, fibromyalgia, lupus) or an unexplained illness have an earthbound energy around them. If an earthbound spirit is manifesting, they are receiving energy from somewhere.

If spirits are earthbound, it is because of a choice they made, usually out of fear of the unknown. This decision can be made because of a sudden death, suicide, wanting to hold onto physical things (like money) on this side, or looking for something or someone on this side, to name a few precise cases. We all have free will, which transcends physical death; we always have a choice. Some earthbound spirits remain because they are fearful of heaven.

When I am called for a session, earthbound spirits may put obstacles in my way, because my car or a client's car to break down, disconnect phones, make time warps, hide phone numbers, or interfere with electricity. It is, therefore, prudent to have a sense of humor and patience when working with earthbound spirits.

Earthbound beings usually have sadness, grief, and a clingy vibration. Many times I see them as dark shadows or shapes, not vibrant, loving beings.

With earthbound spirits, I respect them by finding out why they made the decision to stay here on earth instead of ascending to heaven. If I can, I help them come to peace with those aspects that are keeping them from crossing over. Then I facilitate their journey to the other side.

When sending an earthbound spirit to heaven, any thing in that spirit that is not of God (what you might call evil, or "bad things" that they had done) will burn off in the light of heaven. Think of a dark room. Once you turn on a light, all the shadows dissolve. Darkness, or evil, disappears when the light is turned on.

DIGGING

Some dogs dig as a hobby. They can find it incredibly fun. This usually stems from boredom: they find digging to be the best fun available to them at the time. They may also dig out under a fence to obtain freedom, because they feel alone or bored. My dog Gracie loves a good dig when going after a gopher. Digging can satisfy the "hunting" behavior many breeds have. Dogs also dig because they are hiding treasures and treats. Parceling out less treats so no extras are around to hide can help solve this.

Two different approaches that modify destructive behavior in pets (like digging) are: work with dog trainers to cure or modify the behavior (i.e., for a digging problem take your dog's paws and help them dig in a muddy hole until they develop an aversion to it), or communicate with the dog to understand and mediate a solution that is acceptable to both parties.

CAROL & DAISY

Carol came up to my booth at the Western States Horse Expo, and complained that her dog Daisy constantly escaped the backyard. Carol queried me on how Daisy was able to achieve this.

The picture I received was of Daisy digging under the fence. Carol became incensed. Her dog simply did not dig. I just channel the information I'm given, (repeating the information given to me by the higher view) so I didn't argue with her.

The next morning, Carol was back at my booth. "I went home, and looked around the base of the fence," she said. "Daisy has dug more than thirty holes under the fence! I apologize for the way I treated you yesterday!"

BARKING

Dogs bark because we humans want our dogs to bark.
For years our domestication process and selective breeding has
allowed our dogs to develop their barking abilities.
Wolves don't bark. Barking was further developed in dogs
in order to scare intruders or to help the master out
(i.e., on farms to assist in gathering the sheep).
~ Why Your Shih Tzu Barks

Many clients come to me because their dog is barking too much, too loud, or at inappropriate times. The first thing I do with these dogs is check in to see what they consider their purpose or job is. If their presence on earth is to protect their owner, many of them see it as logical to bark a warning. If they do not have an assigned job from their owners, often barking at the postman, the UPS guy, or anything that moves, is a way for a dog to feel he is helping with the family chores. Many dogs mysteriously stop using their free energy to patrol the fence when they are given a job of carrying a pack on walks, or trained for obstacle course obedience.

A great cure for the barking dog that announces when someone approaches is to thank him or her. Think about it. If you thought your job was to tell your mom there was someone at the door, and your mom just said, "No! Stop!" You'd keep repeating, "But there's someone here!"

Several of my clients take this a step further and give out a treat, saying, "Great job!" Most dogs know the sound of the treat jar, and instantly forget about barking. If you want to give your dog another job, do it. If you continue to employ them as a visitor-noise announcer, rewarding them for a job well done gets them sitting back and relaxing after succinctly completing their job.

Some dogs like to bark when they get together, like a group of teenagers wanting to raise a ruckus. When the neighbor's dogs, Zoë and Daisy, come over to visit my two Bichons, any loud noise outside or on TV will be an excuse for all four of them to run outdoors and bark gloriously. My dogs look quickly around, their eyes dancing, just waiting for an opportunity to spring to action. Let's face it, we humans like to dance and sing and make some noise. We make noise all day talking to each other. Why should dogs be denied the glory of the bark?

Interestingly, wolves do not bark. It is a sound that dogs have learned to make while living with humans.

When communicating dogs will sniff each other, notice where eyes are looking, if heads are down or straight ahead, and will decide whether they need to roll over and show their subservience. Ninety three percent of human communication is non-verbal, so it makes sense that dogs can talk to each other without barking. Still, I hear many dogs do a, "Hey, look over here," bark or "We've got the varmint located in the corner up under the china cabinet." bark. It basically means, "I want your attention, come over here."

When hunting, dogs will bark at a varmint to scare it, or to get it to come out from where it is hiding.

Often I see dogs start barking when there is a shake up or a change in the family's marital status. Brandy, girlfriend of mine, had a dog that had lived with her for several years, without barking issues. Of course her dogs barked when people were at the door, (I would joke it sounded like they were after raw meat) but that was the only barking, when it was time to announce that visitors at the door. Her dogs were Henry, a cocker, and Sassy, a little terrier. When Brandy divorced her husband, Henry fell apart, peed on everything in sight and barked all day while she was gone.

The homeowners' association wrote Brandy up because Henry was barking during the day. She also got a ticket from the police for disturbing the peace. Her solution was to wire Henry with a shock collar—one that sent a strong electric current each time he barked. Every time that I have worked telepathically with a dog that was barking inappropriately, the behavior stopped, making a shock collar unnecessary.

Dogs, cats and horses are not as complex as humans, yet are always sincere. At the very least they deserve to be understood, considering the many hours they spend observing and serving their humans. With good communication (There are many animal communicators available and many, like me, work on the phone), uncover your pet's reason for making noise and strike a compromise. A shock collar that only shocks if the dog is indulging in unwanted behavior is never used, if you have communication and understanding with your dog.

If your neighbor's dog is a nonstop barker, their human is more likely not a caring, responsible pet lover. Or, they could be someone going through a rough patch, needing some help. Get to know your neighbors and see what the actual situation is. The dogs may be bored, lonely, or acting out the intense emotions of the household. Once the reasons are uncovered, the solutions can be found.

PETS AND DIVORCE

When a couple marries, items that belong to each person are brought together into the mutual home. These items will have a charge on them from the people who used them, a charge that carries the intent and emotions felt when used. When couples physically split up they divide their items. If something is kept from the departing spouse, it gives that person (the spouse) the right to visit intuitively or psychically.

Jen had been divorced for five years. Yet she hadn't gotten a good night sleep since her divorce began.

Because of her sleeplessness I questioned if she still had some of her ex-husband's possessions. She did, so we developed a plan to clear the energy in her house, repurpose her husband's items and set an intention to only allow people for her highest good to enter the house.

Pets can feel and see psychic visitations and will often interact with them. They'll growl, bark, meow, look at a space in the room that doesn't seem to contain anything, and set warning borders for protection.

In Jen's case, her dog barked at her ex-husband as he psychically entered her home and while her dog barked every night, she couldn't sleep. Her dog was trying to warn her of unwanted energies (in this case her ex-husband's) and as soon as her house was cleared, the barking stopped.

PSEUDO-ALPHAS

"The only two fears humans have naturally are the fear of loud noises and heights.
All other fears are learned."
~ Elizabeth Kübler-Ross

Over the years, I've worked with a type of dogs that acted erratically or had hard to solve problems. I started calling them "pseudo-alphas." They had been in bad situations and knew that they had been abandoned, or left for dead. They also knew that the person they lived with now had saved their lives. These dogs were not alpha dogs, but were dogs that would be content to follow in second place and stay the course. This can put a lot of stress on an animal that isn't normally an alpha, but feels obligated to protect and serve the human that saved their lives.

Dogs that have been abandoned and turned into a shelter live with a memory and knowledge that other dogs that have always been loved and have a home are without. I find an amazing resiliency in dogs. They are willing and able to let go of fears and move into the present moment if they are asked. This is one of the vast differences between dogs and humans; humans have an almost impossible time of letting go of the past, forgetting their fears, or memories of past harm. Dogs that feel a special calling to a human make a dramatic commitment to that person. It is quite obvious to the dog that if their human's life is threatened, they need to protect them and would sacrifice their lives defending them. Luckily today, few situations call for such devotion and dedication.

Those thoughts are made very real because they have power over reality. With dogs, as with humans, thoughts influence their reality. A dog that comes into the alpha position easily, who feels that they could easily handle anything that comes their way, is surer of their actions and talents. Much like a black belt in Tae Kwon Do who gets in fewer fights than a beginning Tae Kwon Do student, an alpha dog does not attack until absolutely necessary, and when they do, they are confident in their actions.

THE DOG WHO BARKED TOO LOUD

Luke came to me during my first year of practice after his owner, Mary, saw my ad in the local paper. He offered me an invaluable insight into how canines think.

Mary's problem was that when she walked Luke, or whenever they came into view of another dog, he barked hysterically. It was embarrassing to her, and she wanted to modify his behavior. Luke was one of the first "pseudo-alpha" dogs that I had a chance to work with.

He had been a shelter dog, literally rescued from death by Mary. Dogs have a very strong sense of honor and loyalty. For giving him a literal "new lease on life," Luke felt obligated to protect Mary and lay down his life if necessary.

When I asked Luke about his situation, he had an unforgettable response; "Have you seen the size of this place? It's gigantic! There should be at least ten dogs guarding this property! I'm just spread too thin. It's just me here! I'm the only guard! I figure the only chance I have is that when someone comes up, I'll bark really loud. Then whoever is coming up will think there are ten dogs here and will spare us any agony. If I sound like ten dogs maybe the threat will just leave!"

Mary had saved him from death; he felt obligated out of his sense of honor to do whatever it took to protect Mary.

I told Luke that he was safe, that he did not need to worry about protecting his owner. However, I did not know how to break Luke's obsessive thought loop or diminish his barking behavior. Thankfully it was more a nuisance than life threatening.

The real solution was for Mary to be more assertive, which would lessen the burden of protecting her. She could also get a second, more assertive dog, to protect her house and give Luke some time off.

Luke was able to speak his truth, and to be seen as an individual who contributed to the needs of his family, just like his human family members.

ALPHAS AND PSEUDO-ALPHAS

"If your buddy saved you,
And died himself in doing,
Then his courage was not courage,
It was love: love as simple as shaving soap."
~ Anne Sexton, The Awful Rowing Towards God

With most family dogs, they look to their human as a leader and leave the attacking and planning up to them. However, when a dog is aware that his life was saved by a human, sees a situation that could be hazardous, they step up to do the "body guard" thing. This may mean even sacrificing themselves so that their human may live.

Like the codependent that feels they can control an alcoholic's drinking and actions, the pseudo-alpha dog feels that it can control a situation to protect its human and return the favor of saving their life. What I do is surround the pet with guides and angels, clear their life and soul contracts, which helps move them into the present moment. It is better if the dog does not feel so obligated to the rescuer, but there is some "space" around the energy.

My dog Lucie is a prime example of a dog that has been repeatedly abused. I have cleared her energy multiple times, and handled her with loving compassion and awareness. Lucie has been kicked and abused yet she is STILL a people lover. When we are at the dog park, she runs up to people and licks their fingers or legs. If they don't return the affection immediately, she starts scooting (rubbing her bottom on the ground) nervously. When I share why she does this, most people get a soft look on their face and ask how could someone be so cruel. Suffice it to say, that sadly, I know of even crueler people.

Researching the best way to handle Pseudo-Alphas, I turned to *Cesar Milan, the "Dog Whisperer,"* because I wanted a path that was best for all concerned. On his TV show, Milan seemed to solve all situations that came to him. As a dog trainer, he hardly ever gets the back-story that would be available to a communicator.

Cesar is committed to the alpha dog theory and has built a successful career on that belief. With the thousands of dogs I have talked to, not one has stated that they are an "alpha dog"— or even that they are the leader! They'll say to me, "This is my job, I bark and protect." Or, "I give emotional support." Others will say, "I bring laughter into her life."

Cesar Milan talks about "calm assertive energy," and intuitively communicates with the canines in his "pack". Many people interact with animals intuitively without knowing it or acknowledging it. He also works his dogs physically for hours each day, inline skating with them, hiking for hours, or putting them on treadmills. This is a training method commonly used with horses—especially young horses. Exercise a horse by lunging them for 30 minutes and you'll have a much calmer horse.

Temple Grandin, in her book *"Animals Make us Human"*, explains that the alpha dog theory was based on wolves living in captivity that had been placed together as adults. Wild wolves live in families, with a mom, a dad and kids. This is the normal way wolf packs exist in the wild, and that is the way most dogs really are—they live with humans as family. Even if you were the head of a large corporation, you still wouldn't go against your father's wishes, because he still is the head of the household.

Both theories can be true; dogs live in families and dogs thrown together as adults chose an alpha dog leader and have a pecking order. Temple Grandin's belief is that many dogs live in a family. That fits with what dogs and cats tell me; they commonly address their people as family.

OVERWHELMED IN STOCKTON

"Even the tiniest Poodle or Chihuahua is still a wolf at heart."
~ Dorothy Hinshaw

One time while I was in Stockton, California, I talked to a problem dog named Wally. A twenty-five pound Heinz 57, Wally was biting indiscriminately and his life was in jeopardy because of this behavior. He lived with his owner, Tina.

Ted, Tina's son, a married man with two kids, answered the door. When his mother Tina got older, he built an apartment alongside his house for her. The space consisted of a living room, bedroom and a small bath. I was introduced to Tina and Wally. The first thing Tina did was shut the door, leaving her curious son on the other side of it.

The guides showed me that if somebody would come and hug Tina, Wally would get in between and bite them. A person never knew if Wally would be happy to see them or attack them. In his zeal to protect Tina and the "homestead," he attacked indiscriminately.

The immediate vibrational hit I received from Wally was that of a pseudo-alpha. Rescued from a kill shelter, in return, he guarded Tina and her possessions.

Like other pseudo-alphas, Wally talked very fast, repeating himself often.

"I'm supposed to be guarding her, supposed to be guarding her. We had a whole house. I was watching the whole house. Then all of a sudden one day, we're just here. Now we only have three rooms, just three rooms! We used to have a house! I used to have a yard. We had a house! I'm worried. I was apparently asleep at the wheel. I'm worried now that if I do that again we're gonna have just the bed!"

Along with this high-strung communication, Wally also sent me a picture of a bed with four walls around it no available floor space.

He continued, "She's totally gonna lose everything and we're just gonna have a bed. We can't have that, can't have that, so I've gotta be really vigilant and make sure that nobody like sneaks by me, gets one over on me again! Nobody does anything that isn't something that we want done! I know sometimes I get scolded because they don't want me doing what I'm doing but I have to protect her. I must protect her! I have to protect what we have because we lost such a big place! This place is small; we can't afford to lose any more!"

Wally was positive he had to be hyper-vigilant. When I talked to Tina, I found her lonely but graceful. Tina's deceased husband Mark asked to come through immediately. Mark had waited respectfully while Wally talked, but now it was his turn.

Tina showed me a triangular folded flag that had been on the casket after he was killed during World War II. Theirs was a great romantic love story. Mark was in heaven; he spoke of the house he built there for the two of them. Here on earth, they never had a new house together. Mark felt badly about it—after the war, he had promised Tina a home, but had instead died during the middle of construction. Now Mark was keeping that promise in heaven.

He talked of taking dancing lessons so they could dance together when Tina got to heaven. I shared that with Tina and with that admission, she started crying. Tina shared with me that Mark never took the time to learn to dance while he alive. He was keeping his promises, even after death.

A new medium at the time, I was learning that heaven consisted of what we think it is. If we thought of heaven as a place for non-stop bowling and getting drunk, that's what it is. If heaven is all about running in the clouds and playing with dogs, that's what you get. In heaven, dogs frolic on grass, waiting for their humans. I've even seen dogs and horses start a farm or ranch preparing for when their humans come, bonded together again as the family they were on earth. I channel what comes through, but also notice that nothing is too outlandish.

Being poorly behaved, Wally brought a medium to Tina's door. This was a connection that made her the happiest she had been in twenty years; a connection that had also brought through her husband Mark. Dogs create situations for their humans to heal. Many clients who would never normally consult a medium cross my path because of their pets. When animals trust me, it opens their human's heart, and in turn, the client trusts me. That was the case with Tina.

I could feel Tina's ambivalence about being alive. A large part of her wished she were in heaven with her husband, who had been dead for many years. Tina had raised her son alone, and never remarried. Mark was the love of her life. Currently, Wally was her closest friend.

Tina shared with me that her son's wife talked at her like she was an obstacle, something to drag around. Even though Tina lived alongside her son's house, her granddaughter and daughter in-law ignored her. They never shared intimate time together like shopping for clothes or getting their nails done. Most of Tina's friends had already died, and she wondered why she hadn't passed too. Tina's depression and loneliness impacted Wally. Pseudo-alpha dogs often act out when their owners are in emotional distress. Like many humans, dogs are task driven; yet they often feel powerless in the face of depression and grief.

Tina needed to be a part of the family and have a purpose for herself, instead of waiting to die. Taking care of Wally gave her a reason to live, so the talk she heard about shooting him because he tried to bite a few people was devastating.

Spirit guides and Angels came through to Tina with information indicating that she did have a purpose; she also needed to be more assertive about being included in family affairs. Tina said she thought she had been, but realized she needed to be firmer. It became apparent that the children in the family needed the attention and love only a grandmother could give.

I cleared Wally's energy, (see Appendix's on how to do this), then informed him that he was grounded and loved. The angels and guides told Wally they were protecting Tina and the property, so he didn't need to be so vigilant.

Wally's behavior had been pretty severe. After the session, he calmed down some. Tina became more active in her grandkids' lives, knowing she had an important purpose while on earth. She also had a house with a beautiful man that loved her (along with a dance card with her name on it) on the other side.

DOG AND CAT SIBLINGS

Spike had to prove, at least once a week, that he was smarter than the dog. Patsy and I would come back from our walk, and be running down the path to the horse barn. From the side of my eye I saw a furry yellow speedball on a collision course with my fourteen-pound Bichon. Smack! The two of them would collide, Spike arching in a big C to the side and cleanly running away, while Patsy tumbled down the path. I swear I could hear Spike chuckling.

This next practical joke Spike played was even more outrageous.

Six days in a row, Patsy would make me help her look for a varmint in the backroom when we got up in the morning. The first day this happened, I was perplexed, because Patsy was looking under the cat litter box and the file cabinet, places that a mouse would never go. It had to be another creature.

Six mornings in a row, a lizard appeared in the backroom of the house. Patsy could not let another living being alone in our house. She would circle and whine, getting me to move items until she could get at the lizard. Patsy, the great defender of the house, had to make sure she found the creature and neutralize it (Patsy's way of killing varmits was to rap them against the wall as hard as she could).

Finally, Patsy found a lizard. I nabbed it and threw it outside. The next three mornings, we had a repeat of this treasure hunt. But it took an hour out of my day; and scared the crap out of the lizards.

On the fifth morning, I saw Spike bring a lizard into the house and drop it in the middle of the room. Suddenly, I realized what was happening. The lizards were in the back room because Spike was placing them there. After dropping the lizard, Spike got in his cat tree with his paw under his chin and watched the developing hysteria.

Once again, the next day, Spike dropped a lizard in the back room (how was he catching these things so fast?). Again I had to help Patsy find the lizard.

I had a chat with Spike: "You and I both know you are more intelligent than the dog. But I can't take an hour out of each day to help her do this little wild goose chase you set up. I want you to stop bringing in the lizards."

After that simple telepathic conversation, lizards stopped appearing in the house.

ORDER (ALPHA BEHAVIOR) IN CATTLE HERDS

(RURAL ILLINOIS, 1970S)

My Dad planted rye grass in the spring and fall (before and after we planted corn) and we would let the dairy cattle graze in those fields during the day. The Rye was bright green, luscious and smelled of new grass and hope. I would walk out and herd the cattle back into the milk pens. I noticed the lead cow would always be the same. We had two groups of cattle; the milking herd and the dry cow herd (those cows who were not milking for the 3 months before giving birth again). Each herd had their own lead "alpha cow." When a lead cow from the dry herd calved and joined the milking herd, a battle ensued for top cow. Usually this war was over without too much injury.

The alpha pecking order in cattle herds is precise. When bringing the cows in from the field to be milked and walking them back towards the milk parlor they always in the exact same order. The positions never changed with the first cows, the dawdling stragglers at the back, or with any in between. The order was appropriated and decided upon well in advance.

Texas was an aptly named cow, because she had long horns that pointed upward. She was the lead cow of the dry herd, but when she was ready to calf, she was brought into the milking herd. This caused an immediate fight to break out between her and the current lead cow of the milking herd, Bella. Texas lowered her head and charged towards Bella, ripping a large, gaping bloody twenty-four inch diameter hole of a wound in Bella's side.

Texas backed up and charged several more times before we could get the cows separated. Close to being mortally wounded, Bella was lucky to be alive.

My dad was so furious with Texas that, in retaliation, he immediately sawed her horns off, not waiting till after the fall freeze when there are no flies or mosquitoes around. When an adult cows horns are sawed off, you can see directly into their head—the holes can be two inches wide—with all the little nooks and crannies of what, by all appearances, looked like brain matter. Texas seemed vulnerable, an easy mark for an infection to lay claim and kill her. Fortunately, both cows healed. We dedicated ourselves to dehorning calves, so the event wouldn't happen again.

When milking, there were cows that came into the parlor first and stragglers. First cows were well behaved; healthier for the most part, and high milk producers. Many of the stragglers were the "bad girls" who kicked and behaved poorly. It was like high school with the greasers and the preppies.

Unlike beef cattle that have minimal contact with humans, dairy cattle (think black and white Holsteins) have prolonged contact with humans. Holsteins are milked twice a day and can live well into their twenties, making them well versed in the ways of humans. These amazing docile animals are bred to be domestic. Their energy is unlike any other. I feel blessed to have spent so many hours in my life working with our dairy herd. I am also grateful for the energy they add to the world.

FAIRNESS

One of the things I really love about dogs is that when you start giving out treats, they all wait in line. Because they automatically just assume you're going to be just and fair.

Dogs are fair. They will play at another dog's level of skill to be able to play (this has been scientifically proven). Lucie's friend Gizmo (a hundred pound lab) is playing tug of war with her (a 14 pound Bichon) he'll be a lot gentler with her than he would Gracie (who weighs 24 pounds). Because he knows if he isn't fair, Lucie will quit playing and then he won't have anybody to play with. What good is that? It's the fun of the game with dogs, not just winning.

Consistent fairness and specific cues are critical. If you hug a dog when it jumps on you, then the next time scold them, that's how you will create an insecure dog. I have seen dogs constantly on edge because they don't know what is expected. Unpredictable treatment takes away a dog's dignity or enthusiasm for life and can make them downtrodden.

WHAT BEARS MORE INFLUENCE: ENVIRONMENT OR GENETICS?

"Health is a reflection of how we fit into an environment."
~*Bruce Lipton*

There is a broad based genetic experiment occurring with domesticated dogs. People have taken dogs formerly bred for certain tasks and repurposed them. For example, Border collies have been bred and trained to herd cattle for hundreds of years; Bichons were companion dogs; Chinese Shar-Pei guarded their charges. Labradors and golden retrievers as hunting partners went into water. These days, most dogs are simply family companions.

Dogs historically have been breed for certain behaviors, or to have a talent for certain tasks. Just because the badger-hunting wiener dog is now a housedog, doesn't mean that now "badger hunting" energy and talent has disappeared.

The ultimate result of those vast experiments is still unknown. How are these animals going to respond to the new needs of their humans? Dogs seem to be very malleable. Look at all the breeds currently in the world, and then realize that they are all descendants from one type of wolf, even though most breeds do not even look like one another.

Compare the genetic diversity in dogs to the varieties of cats on the planet. While they vary in size, all cats have the same basic nose (with perhaps the exception of the Persian's shorter nose), triangular ears, and similar sized legs. You can easily see that they are genetic relatives. On the other hand, the various breeds of dogs vary greatly in appearance; shape, size, weight, behavior. Has this been evidence for the way dogs try to please humans while cats have been true to themselves?

In genetics, the larger the gene pool, the better adapted the species is likely to be and the population thrives. When the gene pool is smaller, recessive genes that hurt the population may begin to reduce its vigor. Because of diversity, a hybrid (mixed breed) is generally stronger than a purebred. Hybrid animals get the best traits their different species parents; Hybrids (mutts) are unique while allowing inferior recessive traits to not emerge. Plus, they often have the added bonus of being totally adorable!

The new trend is creating designer dogs by breeding different purebreds to each other produces offspring that are novel with endearing traits. This is how the "Labradoodle," "Puggle", "Multipoo," and "Schnoodle" came into being. Farmers have been doing this with livestock for centuries and calling them hybrids.

When choosing a dog, look carefully at your reasons for including the new pooch in your home. Is a purebred dog of value to you? Purebreds are held more true to the standards of their breed. That may be more than what you need in a pet.

If you want a purebred dog you can still get a rescue dog. All breeds have rescues now. A rescue adds the benefits of a pet's profile from the foster parent, and up to date health care.

Mutts are the best kind of dogs; they are unique and one of a kind. Having shown both purebred dairy cattle and purebred Paint horses, I heartily agree that maintaining a pool of genetic diversity in a population while also having a purebred line is of value. Several genetic diseases like HYPP (hyperkalemic periodic paralysis) and Tying–up have been genetically mapped in horses and are being bred out. This is possible because the genetic records having been kept for purebred lines.

Dogs that are planning to reincarnate, sometimes ask to come back as a different breed, perhaps as one that isn't black so they aren't hot in the sun, or as smaller pup so they're allowed on the furniture.

PETS AND THEIR HUMAN'S EMOTIONS

"Dogs are the only species that look humans in the face and change behavior depending on what they see." Temple Grandin

Animals that are empathic for their humans absorb the anger that is in the home. One day, when I was seated outside at a restaurant, I witnessed a woman's pit bull viciously attack another dog who happened to be walking by. The woman grabbed the pit bull and put it in a submissive hold posture. While she was doing this, the guides projected to me that the anger was not the dog's possession; the anger belonged to its owner.

Pets watch their humans explicitly with care. They will base their behaviors on the mood of the owner, sensing when the owner is in pain, tense or unhappy. Much like young children, they can feel a misplaced sense of responsibility for their human's moods, whether good or bad.

This is an important point, because like food dye on a sponge, dogs will soak up our emotions without even thinking about it. As caretaker of the canines that live with us, we need to ground and dispose of our own anger, not allowing it to disseminate to our pets. If it does, tragedies can often occur very easily resulting in the death of the dog.

Projection is way anger and feelings affect our animals. You can think of it like "pass the hot potato"; the game we played as kids. When there is a part of ourselves that we will not own up to, we project it on to others and hold them accountable for what we truly are responsible for ourselves. (I am not angry, my dog is angry.) This is known as the "shadow side" in Jungian therapy. An interesting way to try to cope with this is to make everything *your* fault; because ultimately, you are the only one who has the power to change anything in your household.

ANIMALS AND ANGER

You never, ever correct an animal out of anger or frustration. This is when animal abuse—or child abuse or spousal abuse— occurs. When you try to correct your dog out of anger, you are usually more out of control than your dog is.
~ *Cesar Milan, Cesar's Way*

Anger has no place in a relationship with your animals, and my unwavering rule is that I will not interact with animals from an angry place. Dogs, cats, and horses feel anger immediately, and can respond by going into a fear zone. What may not be instantly apparent is that if you are angry, just being present during that time, will change what experience your animals have.

There are experts who report that animals are mainly fear motivated. I disagree. While some cats and dogs will react to certain situations out of fear, others do not have the word (fear) in their vocabulary. I have determined from experience that dog and cat fears are mostly learned behavior. Abused animals are conditioned by their people to not trust people.

However, some animals are fearless. One example of a lack of fear is my cat Elvis. The only fear I ever saw him display was when I gave him a bath. He is quite obviously afraid of the water, but nothing else.

Elvis sleeps on his back with his toes curled, and utterly adores life. He lets my dog, Gracie; pull him around by his ears. Sometimes, Gracie will have Elvis by the throat. Concerned I will reach down to check that the gagging noise I hear from Elvis is nothing serious. Instead, I find him purring, content to have so much attention from Gracie.

Have you ever witnessed what happens when a threat comes to a non-dominant dog? Instead of attacking, they usually roll over and lay still, showing their soft underbelly. With the exception of the direst of circumstances such as facing a dog with rabies, battles are diverted. Generally no blows are landed, and both parties understand what just happened. Do we humans handle hostile situations so gracefully? Anger in humans can be volatile, causing unnecessary loss, pain and suffering.

I have worked with shelter animals, adopted pets, and pets from horrendous experiences such as Hurricane Katrina or the California forest fires. I have found that fear can be very present in those animal's lives, and can be exacerbated if they have been abused.

The amazing fact is that if you clear the energy on these crisis animals, they almost always drop their fear and transition to present time, totally unafraid.

I have talked to pets that have been kicked, shot, violently hurt and consistently abused. Anger has no place in a home with pets (or children). Adding drug addiction or alcohol to volatile anger is like throwing a match into a can of gasoline.

A closing word about anger. I have never worked with an animal that was purposely malicious. Cats, well, cats will get pissed; then they get even. Once, when I had gone away for ten days over the holidays, my cats got on the shelf above my fireplace and pushed every picture with glass off the ledge. I came home to a living room showered in broken glass. I knew immediately that this was retaliation for leaving them locked in the house alone for so long.

Many of my clients with cats have confirmed the same thing: that many of their issues had to do with cats becoming upset and getting even. In spite of this, though, the cats didn't get carried away. It was more like, "You can't treat me like that, and if you do, this is what happens." It becomes more about setting boundaries than an all-out assault.

SETTING HOUSE BOUNDARIES

If I could give a gift to the dogs of the world, it would be for humans to see their intent. Dogs cannot lie. I have never worked with guard dogs, but even in that instance, a dog doing a job that a human has told them to do. If you realize that the intent of canines is always to please you, then disobedience primarily becomes an issue of communication.

It is fair to have black and white rules of the house; in fact, it is preferred. You wouldn't allow a roommate to leave the toilet seat up, leave old food lying around on the floor, or chew on the couch. Your four-legged roommate needs to also be held accountable.

I believe in the family model of behavior. Think of teenagers. They are always pushing boundaries, trying to get their way. Promote your rules as the black and white rules of the universe. Then the outcome is out of your hands.

Do not repeat yourself over and over when asking for correct behavior. If I ask my dog (or cat) three times to come, sit, or whatever, and they ignore me (by the way, *they hear you*; their life is *focused* around you, and they totally know that they are *choosing to* ignore you), correct their behavior.

It is not always easy to be an enforcer. My horses throw hay into their water tanks to soften it up and have a big hay-fest mess. It dirties the tank, and I have to spend a lot of time cleaning it. The way to prevent this is to feed them far away from the tank, making it difficult for them to carry the hay to it.

Even though I *know* this, some days I am too tired, too moody, or feel like I should just give them what they enjoy, break the rule, and feed them hay next to the water tank. I am the one not being consistent. Yet I come back and yell at them for putting the hay in the water when, in reality, it was a consequence of my behavior.

CREATING SACRED SPACE

Build something into your pet's life that has a positive charge to it (you can do this for yourself as well; see *Wealth Without a Job, by Phil Laut and Andy Fuehl*). This will be an experience that you keep adding good things to, helping to reinforce the relationship with your pet (In *Merle's Door*, it was a song). Patsy and I had a song as well, "Snuggle Puppy." *(Snuggle Puppy! By Sandra Boynton)*. Adding words to music is a great way to anchor positive feelings in your four-legged family.

With my dogs, I do something that I call puppies on the bed. I lie on the bed, rub their tummies, and sing a song about puppies on the bed with much enthusiastic happiness in my voice. It's a very positive experience for all of us and it also grounds me. We come back to a space of love that is ours. It reminds us there's nothing more important in the world. No matter what happens, we are still going to have puppies on the bed and be together. That alone is important, especially to dogs that once did not have a home.

This exercise works if you have a frightened dog. By saying "puppies on the bed," the dog that was barking at the front door comes running for some loving. Because you cannot be in fear and love at the same time, it will help bring a dog away from the edge of fear. My dogs will come immediately because they love doing "puppies on the bed."

With declaration, a sacred space is created, and a sharing of love that is very important for all involved. It's a big gift you can share with your dogs. It shows them that you love them, you care about them, and that they are a priority in your life. It is also something that you can enjoy as well. That is the great thing about dogs; if you are happy, they will be happy too.

By choosing an event and repeating it, you add the aspect of ritual and fun for your dog. Other ideas include creating "Puppies on Parade," a special time in the kitchen or in the back yard, or a walk in sacred space.

Finally, I really suggest that you don't do a sacred space event around food. Contrary to popular belief, not every dog or cat is motivated by food. Also, if they happen to have full bellies when you want to connect with them, they may not respond. Even if they often seem to live for food, they don't all the time. It's good to save food for other motivational needs.

HOW NAMES AFFECT YOUR ANIMALS

At a horse show, Diane shared with me how she obtained her latest dog. Driving home, she found a lump of fur on the road, lying motionless on the yellow line between the lanes of asphalt. She stopped and was amazed to find that it was a young puppy, unharmed and no worse the wear for being on the centerline of the highway.

Diane decided to call the pup, Speed bump, a metaphorical reference to where he was found. Diane used "Bump" for short. When I talked to Bump, he told me he *hated* the name. He shared with me that every time he heard "Bump" he relived his horrible experience, falling out of a truck and landing on the pavement, with the added horror that the people he belonged to didn't come back to get him. They didn't even notice he was gone.

Luckily, Diane came along and saved him. He suffered post-traumatic stress from the ordeal, which was triggered again every time someone said his name. I cleared the little guy's energy, and Diane renamed him Sammy.

BIG HEAD CAT

Tamara loved to dress her cat for holidays. She especially likes July, fourth, when she put a big hat, leggings and long grey beard on her cat Big Head. Tamara called me to talk about some very specific issues concerning Big Head.

But in the back of her mind, was the most important question of all; does Big Head like being dressed up in clothes? Tamara had thought a lot about it, and if Big Head said he hated being dressed up, she would stop doing it. But she didn't want to, it was the absolute best time she had with Big Head, just incredible fun.

Cats hate restrictive clothing. However many cats confide in me that they tolerate dress-up because they love the attention. Remember, cats have a healthy sense of humor and like to be the center of things. There was a reason that the Egyptians called cats the "gods of joy."

Because of Big Head's love for Tamara, he wanted to get dressed up, and please her. He loved the attention he got when she put his clothes on. He enjoyed the continued adoration he received afterwards showing off his wardrobe. It was a fair exchange in his mind.

ELVIS

Some animals will ask for a name, as my cat, Elvis, did. He didn't just say what he wanted to be called; he presented a case for *why* he should be called Elvis. He shared that he was one of a kind, had black hair and wanted to be known as "The King".

I blanched slightly at sharing my house with a cat so conceited he wanted to be called "The King". Luckily, Elvis has a heart of gold, so it doesn't come off as conceited, just fact. I would have never named a cat Elvis on my own, but after knowing him, I can't see him having any other name. In the years since giving him that name, I have found that he has a propensity to be a "Fat Elvis". He loves to sing; growling and whining easily because "there just aren't' enough happy vocal tones".

Some names are chosen in haste, like the names that rescuers give dogs before they are adopted. My BichonFurKids (the name of the rescue group I adopted from) came with "Calisa" and "Carissa"; names I could hardly say, let alone spit out multiple times a day when calling them.

When I adopted them, Lucy's name came forward immediately. She has apricot hair on her forelock and down her back, and the red hair reminded me of Lucille Ball. Nothing came to me immediately for Gracie, so I called her Desi (yes, I realize that was not a good choice for a girl dog). It was a few weeks before the name "Grace" came through. It fits her perfectly; she is so loving and God-given. Her name also reminds me to be in the grace of God.

As with Bump, some names actually cause trauma in your animals, others bring out qualities that may not be desired. I gave my horse the barn name, Rowdy, after Clint Eastwood's character in the old TV show, *Rawhide*. My horse is feisty. With that name, people expect him to act up and many times he does. Many animals will live up to a name, or grow into it, just as they become more like your perceptions of them.

Take the time to pick a desirable name. When I was teaching Tae Kwon

Do, my partner and I would sometimes pass someone on to a higher rank, because they would "grow into the belt." With that in mind, name your pet something that they can grow into, that aspires to greatness or, at least, individuality. Provide each of them with a name that will serve them well their entire lives.

When I'm working intuitively, information comes through regarding the name of the pet (or a person). All that is necessary is the first name of the animal, and then I add the last name of their human parent. A name is very important. So give the naming of your animals some serious thought.

A SPECIES IN A NAME

Sarah sat down for a session, and I tuned into the energies around her. An animal came through for her, shape shifting between a cat and a dog. Finally the animal told me he was a cat, but he had a lot of dog traits and identified with the lifestyle of a dog. He told me he had the purpose of a dog. When I shared this with Sarah, she replied: "Of course he would come through that way! We called him CAA-Dog!"

DEATH AND DYING

When my best friend had her breast cancer reoccur the third time before she was forty, I became interested in what happens when we die. I attended Anne and Larry Lincoln's workshop on death and dying based Elizabeth Klubler Ross's work. I remember that they brought in a man from Australia that had experienced a near death experience. Everyone in the workshop crowded around him and was entranced by the information. Today near death experiences are much more common, and more people are becoming to believe that they are possible.

Many times the same people who tell me they don't believe in afterlife and that mediums are fake are the same people who ask me to talk to their pets on the other side. It seems many people think there are different rules governing animals and people. When I first started, about once a week I would have someone become agitated and irate at me, angrily sharing that they did not believe that dogs/cats have souls. Today I do not remember the last time that belief was expressed to me. While it could be that I am just exposed to different people, I believe that the public opinion of life after death and which beings are sentient is rapidly changing.

This section discusses my own interactions with beings dying, along with clients experiences that have impacted my beliefs. We are close to our animal family members, and how we handle their passing affects how we handle our own beliefs about death.

DEAD IS DEAD

(RURAL ILLINOIS, 1970'S)

It was a spring that never came;
But we have lived enough to know
That what we never have, remains;
It is the things we have that go.
~ Sara Teasdale

On a farm, being romantic about death is a luxury. The first thing to do everyday at the housing where the hogs were confined was to walk through and throw out the dead pigs. Because they are so slight, baby pigs can get dehydrated and die quickly. Many times in birth, especially with large litters of up to 18, runts have little chance of surviving and several might be born dead.

When I took animal science in college, I was stunned when I learned about the acceptable death rate for raising hogs. Though ours was one fourth of that rate, my dad still blamed someone (which meant either my mother or me were the ones held responsible.) every time an animal died.

During my childhood those farm animals constantly lived under the torrent that was my father's wrath. My father didn't outright kill anything, but he would smack a cow with a hammer or try to poke a sow's eyes out with teeth cutting pliers because she wouldn't go into a crate. My father was an original. What stymies me is that he never learned that by beating up the animals he didn't get as much milk, or as much cooperation.

Because I belonged to 4-H, the animals that were mine had to be owned by me. My father took advantage of this, and sold baby Holstein heifers to me for fifty dollars, a lot of money at the time. Of course, I never paid for grain, hay or board, so it was really more complicated than that. But as far as I was concerned, they were my cattle and Dad called them mine also.

In all my years with my father, I never remember a time where he took responsibility. Anything disastrous on the farm was either my fault or my mother's fault—he never even chalked stuff up to accidents or acts of God. If he felt badly about going off the deep end screaming one day, he would hand me twenty or forty bucks the next day, depending on the severity and his guilt. He never apologized.

My dad was never a written records guy, although he had an incredible memory. I was consumed with the idea of showing and competing with dairy cattle, but I couldn't do it with my Dad's herd because they were considered grade (i.e., not registered) Holsteins. When I found out later that when building his herd he had bought registered cattle and just let the registration papers go, I was incredulous. I always felt like our cows were second-class citizens, because they weren't properly registered Holsteins.

My big break came when the Whiteside County 4-H held a letter writing competition to win a baby heifer calf. You wrote a letter on why you should have the calf, and then a committee picked the best letter. The idea was that after she grew up and had her first baby heifer that offspring would then go back to the letter writing program so another 4-H'er could win a calf. As it turned out, I won the contest. It was a stroke of luck for me and it became the first time I had my picture in the paper.

My brother-in-law helped me write the letter, and while I wanted to say I deserved to win because I had never won anything (going on the premise that if I had never won anything, it must be my turn), my brother-in-law made me list all the reasons I deserved to have the calf, and how nice I would treat it when it became mine. There was another caveat to winning the contest; I had to have the calf registered as part of the 4-H project. At the time I didn't realize the significance of this, but with the benefit of hindsight it explains a lot regarding why Dad let me join 4-H.

4-H as it turned out, changed my life and saved me in many ways. It gave me access to much needed friends, projects which I could call my own and excel in, and time away from the farm. My father allowed it, even though he didn't like me to be absent from chores.

Almost every day when I walked up the lane from the bus, my Dad met me to ask what my grades had been that day. He never failed to mention that I was going to college. Somehow, later, I associated going to college along with being in 4-H. The public speaking, demonstrations, and all the awards I won set me on the path of a career achiever.

Rules took total control over my life. Written rules,: 4-H showing registered cattle; unwritten rules: I had to get A's each day in school; unspoken rules- nothing was ever Dad's fault, and you didn't criticize him—took total control over my life. The most detrimental zinger of them all was my father saying, "If I had your luck in raising livestock, I'd be bankrupt. All your animals get sick and die."

I tied Bonnie, the "contest calf," to a metal fence post while the start of the pen she was to live in was being built (My father never let me keep cattle that were going to be shown with the rest of our herd. He thought it was how disease could be spread.). While tied, Bonnie jumped the wire panel and ended up with the fence post sticking through her side. Sixty some stitches later, she was given a cautious prognosis. She seemed to heal, and we went ahead and bred her to become part of the dairy herd. Even though our Holstein cattle were not registered, breeding was done by artificial insemination, and all of those bulls were registered. So it was easy to breed Bonnie to a registered Holstein bull. She had twins, giving me the jackpot of having one calf to give away, and another to keep. Luckily, she had two heifers (because with a boy and a girl, the female would usually be barren).

Bonnie got sick after the birth, and we had her in the barn while we waited for the vet. Inexperienced, and not knowing that we treated our own livestock, the vet assumed the cow in the barn was who he was called for. He treated her with sulfa, before he talked to us—giving her an additional dose over what we had already given her. Bonnie had a reaction, and swelled up with big welts all over her body. She was critically ill for several days, and then seemed to recover.

We milked Bonnie and rebred her. I was fifteen when she aborted at seven months pregnant. Apparently Bonnie hadn't recovered totally from the overdose of sulfa (it wasn't until Veterinary Science in college that I would learn that sulfa toxicity leads to kidney failure) and as a result, she could not carry a full term pregnancy. With the abortion she became critically ill. Until this time I had never lost a calf or cow, and I didn't know what the signs were of an animal being close to death. Available Veterinary Science books all maintained that any disease could end in death, but I didn't much firsthand experience. Such was my naïveté regarding bovine diseases.

I had an event scheduled for that night, a meeting at the high school. I couldn't drive yet, so I valued my small social life and wanted to go, if at all possible. I asked Dad if he would watch Bonnie and stay up with her if she got worse, then headed off. When I returned home, Bonnie was dead.

I was devastated. I felt sure at the time that if I had stayed by her side, she would still have been alive. I cursed my shortsightedness, putting a social schedule above my cow's life. I felt the type of guilt that I would spend decades perfecting: that of making the wrong decision for an animal in my care, which leads to their death.

I felt so horrible, I asked my dad for special treatment of Bonnie's body. What we usually did with cattle carcasses was to have the rendering works pick them up and dispose of them; we were out of the picture at that point. Instead, I begged my dad to bury Bonnie on the farm. To give a decent burial like the member of the family that she was.

I thought my father agreed to this a little too readily—and I don't know if it was that he saw the absence of logic with my plan, really wanted to be nice to me, or just wanted me to stop crying. I took Bonnie's death hard. A human being has some say in their own medical treatment, whereas animals are at our mercy.

Dad agreed to bury Bonnie in the woods, along where he parked farm equipment that was outdated. I was relieved, until reality set in. It was January, with a solid freeze and snow on the ground in northwest Illinois. My father wrapped Bonnie's legs with log chains, then dragged her body behind the tractor to the crest of the lane and left her by my horse's pen.

Twice a day when I fed my horses, I got to stare at Bonnie's glassy eyes and lifeless, bloated body. The ground was frozen hard, and we had to wait until the spring thaw to dig, especially considering a hole large enough for a 2000-pound body. The body froze too. If I had realized how long it would be before Bonnie would be buried, I would have somehow found a tarp and covered her. But I didn't.

After looking at a ton of dead cow twice a day, with her staring back at me with motionless eyes, I made a decision. "Dead is dead. I am never going to be sentimental about the disposal of a body again". Another conclusion came to me that harsh spring; whatever it was that made Bonnie, Bonnie; it left long before the carcass was ever buried.

TALKING TO THE DYING

"Birth, death and suffering all bring us to the very edge of what our minds can understand." ~ Ram Dass

For me, embarking on the adventure of talking to animals on the other side was comparative to Columbus sailing forth on the Atlantic Ocean. One day the world was flat, and you could sail right off the edge. The next, there were new lands with riches not even imagined before, and inhabited by people with strange cultures. I read everything I could get my hands on in those days, but the information wasn't always accurate. My particular field seemed devoid of experts, and though I searched for a mentor in animal communication, I could not find one. With an M.S. in Animal Science and a lifelong relationship with them, I felt comfortable with all aspects of cats, dogs, horses, and cattle. With guidance from my spirit guides and angels, I plunged in, started to gather evidence, and learn commonalities, with one very important point: I could hear the angels and spirit guides every step of the way.

What happens when pets die? I have knowledge built from mediumship experience, faith that represents feelings. But faith lends itself to dogma and we can't pass feelings around the room like we can photographs. Feelings can be shared, but not totally comprehended in the same exact way for each individual. Feelings are a sense of knowing that cannot be adequately described to another, hence, ideas and concepts arising from these feelings gravitate into the dogma of the subject, in this case, the death of a pet.

Unlike humans, it appears that animals do not go through a life review, and become available to contact immediately after death.

The Universe runs with a precision that comes from order, and with order there are rules. A protocol, if you will. The only way to discover these rules is to observe how the Universe operates.

PATSY'S INNER WISDOM

Patsy had innate abilities to discern illness. When working a crowd, she always went to the most vulnerable, ill person first. Her commitment was apparent immediately; she loved on everyone, no matter how disgusting or unlikable the person may first have appeared. Initially she chuffed harshly at the smells on smokers, but subsequently learned to hold back her reactions long enough to work seamlessly with them as well.

On a summer's afternoon; Patsy was deep in thought: she ran out our house's front door and bee lined across the street to Freddie's house. Freddie was a neighboring Chihuahua that was Patsy's occasional walking partner.

Freddie's human mom, Alice, came out and shared with us that Freddie had come down ill earlier. Two days later, Patsy bolted over to Freddie again. Much to my surprise, Freddie had passed just a few hours before. Patsy went to pay her respects.

Whenever I traveled, Patsy stayed with her best friend, Bobby, a black Lab. One day, Patsy sent me a mental image telling me she wanted to see Bobby. When the two of them were together that day, a feeling passed over me that Bobby was getting ready to leave this world. We spent time with her, honoring what a great friend she was to both Patsy and me. A few days later, Bobby was dead.

SPEEDY CAT'S PASSAGE

Put the rubber mouse away,
Pick the spools up from the floor,
What was velvet shod, and gay,
Will not want them, any more.
What was warm is strangely cold.
Whence dissolved the little breath?
How could this small body hold
So immense a thing as Death?
~ Sara Henderson Hay, collected in: Reflections on a Gift of Watermelon Pickle

My becoming an intuitive coincided with my cat Speedy getting older. When Speedy started meowing loudly during the night, I chalked it up to the beginnings of senility. A particularly astonishing case made me realize that what was actually going on was that Speedy was meowing at the spirit energy that was in the house at night. I cleared and protected the house, and the meowing stopped.

When he turned twenty-six, Speedy started looking rougher than usual. I got the sense that he would be passing soon. He had been my companion for over two and a half decades and I wanted to do right by him.

I asked Speedy if he wanted help leaving the planet. He seemed not to be coherent some of the time, so I put it in terms we would both comprehend. I told him that he had never once pooped on the carpet in the house his whole life. If he wanted assisted suicide, tell me by defecating on the carpet. That would be a sure sign that he wanted to bow out. Although I can easily converse with other people's animals, talking to my own is more difficult, because I don't have the distance or impartiality.

We had this conversation on a Thursday morning. The following Tuesday night, he lay on the bathroom floor, dying. For the previous five days he had pooped on the floor, and I had done nothing (other than clean up the mess). Now, at two in the morning, for the first time ever, Speedy did not purr while I stroked him. He was suffering and I was unable to intercede. Troubadour, who is my singing spirit guide, was humming "Suicide Is Painless," the theme song from *M*A*S*H*. Speedy told me he would not die with me watching, so I was just increasing his suffering by staying up with him. I went to bed. When I woke up four hours later, Speedy was dead, his body becoming stiff.

Several months later, Patsy and I were getting a canine nutritional consult from two ladies at a health food store. One of them was surprised to start channeling Speedy. He was telling jokes and in the high fine spirits of someone in heaven. He positively glowed with joy and humor. The joke was two-fold, because the woman channeling him didn't believe channeling was possible. Speedy took special joy in this—upping the ante and making her squirm. I walked away from the experience knowing that Speedy had made it to heaven and was enjoying every minute of it.

I now thank Speedy for those final gifts: confirmation he understood what I said and the gift of knowing that what I was doing, (talking to him), confirmed that I absolutely could talk to animals.

PATSY BEFORE

I received an email that had a video attached about an old white dog looking over his life. The clip ended with, "You know my eyes are going bad; I've got pretty blurry vision now. I'm coming to the end of my life." I started crying uncontrollably. I looked at Patsy asleep next to me on the couch. What was wrong with me, Patsy was only ten! I would have another decade with her. It struck me how upset the video made me, but I didn't know why. This was three days before her death.

The next day, a photo of animals fell off the wall, the glass breaking. It had hung unperturbed for twenty years. A harbinger of what was to come.

The night before Patsy died, I picked her up at my friends who were dog sitting. She was seated at the kitchen table across from where I stood. Patsy started whining, got up on the table, and then walked across it towards me. She had never walked on a table so it was very strange behavior. She had never whined at me. Only in retrospect did these things make sense.

LEAP DAY, 2008

On the freakiest day of the year, leap day 2008, a most uncommon and bizarre accident occurred early in the morning. I ran out to feed my horses during a television commercial. At the time, I had three horses at home: Mike, Pee Wee and Rowdy. Pee Wee was still a young horse, under two years old, and Mike was the alpha horse, vicious about protecting his food. In fact, Mike could be a down right jerk when it came to food.

Patsy never learned to have a healthy respect or fear of horses. To her they were family, and she felt safe with family. When the vet came out for a sick horse, Patsy liked me to hold her at eye level with them. She would whine until I picked her up. When she could see our faces, she would be immediately engrossed in the conversation.

She thought of the horses as hers, and felt responsible for them. When I asked people how they taught their dogs to stay away from these big animals, I was told that once the dog got stepped on or kicked, they would give them wide berth. However, only 15 pounds, Patsy might not survive such an encounter. That "warning encounter" never happened.

Every morning when I fed the horses, Patsy ran the perimeter of the horse pen and barked, which she included in her job description. It was her way of telling the coyotes that they better stay away from her property and her horses.

Patsy ran ahead of me on that day, barking as usual. I don't even remember why I was standing where I was when the incident occurred, but I will never forget what I saw. The horses had three large flakes of hay spread out in front of them. I then saw Mike bite at Peewee, and Peewee pivot a three quarter turn, dodging the attack. In the meantime, Patsy had happily walked between them with her "I'm a dog on duty" walk.

Pee Wee came down hard on Patsy's shoulders with both front feet. As soon as it happened, Patsy crumpled in a way that I immediately knew she was critically injured. It was apparent that my horse had just killed my dog in front of my eyes.

I frantically ran to Patsy. Physically, she looked normal, although the fur and skin on her chin was torn, hanging down in a flap. I picked her up and was shocked to feel her heart still beating. It gave me hope. "Wow, there's a chance here." I thought.

It's hazy as to how I actually recruited a neighbor to drive us to the vet's clinic two minutes away. I held Patsy gingerly until we arrived, sobbing and asking every angel I knew to make it right.

In the clinic, they put her on oxygen and IV's. A sledgehammer horse hoof had demolished her body; still I was told by the clinic her condition was guardedly optimistic. Patsy was still breathing and had no broken bones.

The accident happened at ten a.m. All day we waited for Patsy to rally. The clinic tried to get her stabilized, but nothing worked, and her brain stem continued to swell. At five o'clock that afternoon, it was decided to transfer her to another facility ten minutes away that had overnight care. Fragile, Patsy now needed to be on a respirator.

At the surgical hospital, there was no improvement. Distraught, I called Unity church prayer hotline, asking them to pray for her all night. I also called a few friends, asking what I should do. An Intuitive friend told me: "you will know; you'll know; when it's absolutely imperative that she has to go, or if she wants to go, you'll know."

At midnight, the Veterinary Surgical Hospital's staff told me to go home. They said that Patsy was stabilized as much as possible, and that they would call me if anything happened. Since I could only see Patsy ten minutes out of every hour, I felt useless there anyway. Obviously, I wanted to be with Patsy constantly, but since I couldn't, I gave in to their advice and went home around twelve thirty.

I received a call three hours later saying Patsy's pupils were blown (in a human body that is considered brain dead). The vet told me that they could continue with life support, but he didn't really know what the purpose would be. One hour later, I was standing at her bedside as Patsy was taken off life support. Her amazing, strong heart kept beating for forty-five minutes after the respirator had stopped.

Without Patsy I was grief stricken and bereft. The world was fuzzy cotton, my nasal passages had permanently swelled, and my eyes were red and sore. I wanted a reason, some ownership of such tragedy. I had let Patsy eat cat food, play in the streets off leash, chase coyotes even, and in the end none of that mattered.

I found comfort going to a Sufi Healing Center. They wafted healing prayers in Arabic towards me. The Sufi's told me I was incredibly beautiful when I cried. I thought to myself, "Well, that's great," because I felt like I was going to be crying for a long time.

I didn't understand what the Sufi's were saying. But they let me cry. I knew enough about grief that I understood that I needed to hit as far to the bottom as I could—to experience it as fully as possible. I wanted to embrace my grief, and being a medium was no consolation. I simply wanted my dog back. After ten years of constant companionship, I missed the physical body of my dog.

Two days after Patsy died, my brother called me to let me know that my mother was sick, not expecting to make it through the week. Bedridden, but not in her usual Alzheimer's fog, she died four days after Patsy. I was in such a stupor that I had not even flown home to be with my mother when she crossed.

Moments after my mothers passing I received more information on the event from my guides. They reminded me that my mother and I had said our goodbyes, which had been necessary because the Alzheimer's soul flits to heaven long before the body is relinquished. There is always a reason for that type of passing.

I had talked it out with my mother's soul months before. I knew what her situation entailed. My guides reassured me if I needed to be at her deathbed, I would have been. In my absence, my brother stood that watch. He could face his fear of death by being our mother's companion on her final journey home.

PATSY AFTER DEATH

A year after Patsy's death, when I was in Mexico riding on a bus to a Mayan ruin, I felt Patsy's spirit energy come back to me, go in behind me and lift me up. It was the most amazing feeling I have ever had: she was showing me her "angel-ness", an all white light of lifting joy. I was crying with tears streaming down my face. I looked around thinking I was making a scene of myself, only to notice that the woman across the aisle was streaming tears too. She said, "It is all so amazingly beautiful." I realized she had felt it too.

Six months after Patsy died, I adopted two Bichon rescues, Gracie and Lucie, who lean backwards into people and put their heads on a person's heart chakra. I never taught them that, and thought, well, maybe all dogs are capable of that; at least those dogs with me. However when I tried to get Daisy, the neighbor dog, to lean over backwards out of my arms, she got uncharacteristically upset with me. Apparently, it isn't something every dog does. Patsy left her legacy to be carried on with my two new girls. How had they learned the technique? I don't know, but I have learned to live more easily with magic and mystery in my life.

CHOICES, GUILT AND GRIEF

"Some of you fear,
That when you die,
There will be an awesome tribunal,
Sitting in judgment upon you.
The truth of the matter is,
That the first thing you see,
When you leave your bodies is Light,
The first thing you hear is laughter,
And the first thing you feel is,
Love."
~ Emmanuel, Book One

While in my twenties my boyfriend lost his dog to Parvo, and became so despondent, he didn't work for weeks. At 24, it was the first time he had witnessed death. On a livestock farm, death happens daily, as commonly as washing your face or feeding the cattle. Now, as a medium, I know without doubt that while the physical body may have died the spirit still exists.

If you have animals in your life, sooner or later you will also know tragedy. Their lives are sped up; what takes humans 70 or 80 years to experience, takes animals only ten to twenty. When my first horse died, I considered it bad luck; isn't that what we call it when we die before our time?

I was in my early twenties when I had a childhood horse die of colic.

Then I lost the replacement horse a year later and I was bereft. This second death was an accident and I blamed myself, because I had been riding with a loose cinch. I had ridden my mare under a tree and leaned to her side, which shifted the saddle. When I tried to straighten it, I couldn't. I stepped off into the left stirrup, and the saddle slid went under her, causing me to land on my butt just a few inches away from my mare's dancing feet.

I was shaken when I realized her hooves were just a few inches away from my vulnerable stomach. In a split second I let go of the reins, incomprehensibly thinking she could easily step on me if I didn't. She galloped down the wash and out onto the asphalt of the adjacent street. A neighbor saw the whole thing, and laughed, "It looks like you could use a lift!" He offered, and I got into his truck.

We drove down the street and after going over a small hill, saw my horse standing in the middle of the road, next to two people who were in front of a motor home that was in the opposite lane. I immediately knew something was wrong. She never would have gone to strangers. However, I couldn't see her feet. Then to my horror as I came around the truck, I saw her left foot almost completely severed, hanging by a mere two inch strip of flesh. She had to be humanely put down.

I never have known for sure how that foot was sliced off at the pastern. There were two possibilities; the first that she had been running on pavement as a two year old (two year old horses still have more fragile bones) and incurred a stress fracture, or, what probably was the culprit; The inch wide cotton training reins that were drenched in blood had gotten stepped on, and then the leg that tried to go thru the stationary rein was sliced neatly off.

I didn't like that second version because it involved a choice that I had made. I had bought those reins, and thought they were soft and large, not realizing they were thick and strong, and wouldn't break if they were stepped on.

After the mare died, I would reprimand myself if I started to feel happy. How dare I be happy when I was indirectly responsible for the accident that led to her death? By punishing myself that way, I stayed in the space of grief where contacting the joy of heaven was impossible. I held on to the misperception that I needed to suffer for what I had done. In an inexplicable way, it also made her feel more alive to me. The pain and guilt were the last things I had of her to hold on to.

I lost two horses in two years, or two over a period twenty years. The later sounded better. I was so distraught, I had nightmares about having another of my horses die, causing me to go insane and be hospitalized. I relived the letting go of the rein again and again.

The next horse I bought after this, I kept at a trainer's and did not take the responsibility of feeding him or riding him alone. I lived in fear of losing another horse.

Since that death, since working this job of talking to animals on the other side, I have since seen the "look of guilt", the feeling that things could have been done differently in the faces of thousands of clients.

Guilt over the death of a pet can far outweigh the grief that we feel from their passing. My observation on this is that while humans sometimes make their own end of life decisions, animals are dependent on us for their care and health decisions. Many times these choices leave us doubting ourselves, second-guessing what could have been. Another sticking point is being with the animal at the end, or taking their care seriously.

If I could give a gift to those bereft of loss, it would be the FEELING of JOY that animals and people experience on the other side. Whatever choices were made on earth, all is forgiven, all forgotten when the spirit transitions. I have never experienced an animal on the other side that held their human responsible or blamed them for the turns that destiny held.

The odds are (and the reality is) that horses do not live as long as people. Horses have a tendency to have really, incredibly bad things happen to them. They have a brain the size of a walnut, 180 feet of intestines and are incapable of throwing up. Tragedy is part of the deal.

That is what really happens. There is the loving and there's the releasing of that period of your life being finished. The love is still there. There's the joy because the love was there in the first place. We can't feel that when we're in grief. This might not even be apparent in several stages of grief.

Early in my training, I was taught that animals that love us are with us more when they are on the other side, because they are no longer anchored to their physical bodies. Yet when faced with the loss of a pet, knowing that they are still connected in spirit does not always ease suffering.

Now I can feel the love of all of the beings that I have shared my life with. This is comforting and freeing at the same time. We cannot disconnect ourselves from an animal's love even if we try. It is the blood that flows through our cells, the blood that takes the oxygen of life from the lungs and feeds it to the hungry cells and our spirit.

If death is a transitory state of physicality, then suffering becomes more of an issue. While death is inevitable, suffering need not be. With humans, suffering may be chosen beforehand, through free will. However the guides have drilled it into my head that we are here to experience free will. Nothing is written in stone, we can always make another choice. I have witnessed animals that chose to suffer out of their love or devotion to their humans.

MAGIC AND THE BABIES

My heart broke and laughter fell out.
~ Beatrice Woods

I bought my horse Magic as an unbroken two year old and took her to a neighboring trainer who specialized in youngsters. Magic was a fast learner, winning buckles in several fall futurities in both Western Pleasure and Hunter Under Saddle. Unfortunately at three, she severed a tendon and was unable to collect. I took her home for a new career as brood mare and trail horse.

Magic had several babies for me, but heartbreak visited us too often; we lost foals two years in a row. The first of these babies was a beautiful boy, a loud paint, with a gorgeous body. The first week of his life, he kept trying to urinate, then would expel just a small amount of fluid. At three days old, he got septic (a blood born infection) and almost died immediately.

His bladder had ruptured during birth, so his urine was being released into his body cavity. We took him to a veterinary surgical clinic, which conducted emergency surgery to repair the tear. The surgery was successful. Even though exhausted by the ordeal, Magic and her son recuperated. Then the day before the pair was to return home, his bladder ruptured in another area, and he abruptly died.

I rebred Magic to the same stallion, being told such a horrible birth defect couldn't happen twice. Unfortunately, that wasn't true. The next year

Magic had a baby who looked healthy, at first glance. The foal had been alive for almost a half hour when I realized that he had scoliosis and his whole body was arced like a parenthesis. I went to bed that night, praying to God that his will be done, (this was before I knew I was psychic) and that I be shown what I should do with this disfigured being.

I woke up early and ran out to Magic's stall. She nickered softly when she saw me and lifted her head to me. Then she nudged the baby that was lying on her feet. When I looked towards the baby, I almost wretched. He was calmly lying on the straw, with most of his intestines out of his body.

I ran back into my house and called the vet. We humanely put the foal down. Magic and I fell into a deep grief.

A week after the baby's death, I saddled up Magic and we went trail riding. We were walking along the path going into an arroyo, with the bright blue Arizona sky and a slight breeze lifting the air. Anyone who saw us would think that we made a beautiful pair and would assume that we didn't have a care in the world. Obviously, that was not the emotional space either of us was in.

However, when she took that first step on the sand of the wash, Magic lifted her head. She then shook her head and shuddered, a movement that, to me, meant that she was shaking off the weight of the world. She raised her head again and gave it a little flip, saying, "C'mon. Let's play. We are not the ones who are dead." I lifted the reins and clucked to her. We took off running down the wash, the wind brushing off the cobwebs of grief that had been shackling both of us.

I learned from Magic through these deaths. When they came, she grieved deeply and felt the loss firsthand. Magic had given birth to three healthy babies previously and had always had her babies when I was away; priding herself on her capacity to be a strong, loving and efficient mother. These deaths battered the face of those beliefs. However, she knew that in the present moment, it was her task to go on and that the purpose of life is to enjoy it.

Loss can either crack you open or cause you to shut tight and circle the wagons; the way a cat sleeps upon itself in a small circle or an earthworm curls up when exposed.

Grief can sit like a fog upon us. We can no longer feel the connection to our loved ones. Time becomes irrelevant. If you do not deal with grief, it will be there years later. You have to ACTUALLY GRIEVE, to move through your emotions and feel them. People have to grieve the loss of a beloved animal. When I feel intense angst in my chest during an intuitive session, a pet that is being held on the earthbound plane by their human's grief often causes it.

Although beliefs are changing, the death of a pet is not honored by society, as is the death of a human family member. Many people have their pet as the main relationship in their lives, but by not honoring their grief surrounding a pet's death, the message society sends is "you are marginalized." By saying "it's just an animal," the honor sacredness deserving a life of love and sharing is denied.

ZEUS AND APOLLO TAKE FLIGHT

Nobody has ever measured, not even poets, how much the heart can hold.
~ Zelda Fitzgerald

When an animal dies and leaves behind a sibling or dear friend, the communication between the two of them does not necessarily cease. My Kahuna, Candace, had two giant Mastiffs, Zeus and Apollo, that were close friends. Zeus got sick and passed quickly, leaving Apollo alone. Candace called me a few weeks later, asking for advice and a solution.

Apollo had nothing really wrong with him, but he was struggling to stay on this side. When I asked Zeus to talk to me, he came through immediately, very willing to talk. The two of them were totally despondent without each other. Even though Zeus was dead and in heaven, they were still in constant contact.

Zeus shared his version of heaven and showed me that he had amazingly green grass to endlessly run on. The grass was thick, lush, and beautiful. Even the smell of it wafted to my nostrils. The sky was a shade between azure and turquoise and a few clouds meandered across. Trees lined up at the horizon, in a darker yet more subdued green.

Apparently the only thing missing from this amazing heaven was his best friend Apollo. To remedy this, Zeus was sending Apollo a constant stream of pictures of his utopia. Apollo was already saddened and grief-stricken, and the barrage of information from Zeus was creating a mood that undermined his will to live.

I tried to get the message through to Apollo that both he and Zeus had come to this earth with a purpose that was specific for each dog. Both dogs were charged with guarding Candace, and she still needed Apollo. But he felt inadequate guarding Candace alone, since he had always been part of a team. As much as I tried to encourage Apollo that he was quite capable, apparently I didn't get the point across. Two weeks later he was dead.

ADVICE ON WHAT TO DO WHEN GRIEVING FOR A PET

Happiness has a hard time entering a closed heart.
~ Walt Disney

People grieve in many different ways. Know that nothing is unusual. I trained in the "Growth and Transition" workshops of Elizabeth Kübler-Ross, learning how to process events in life. She defined the seven stages of grief: shock, denial, bargaining, anger, guilt, sorrow and acceptance.

Many pet owners get stuck in denial and guilt, sometimes for years. Horse owners in particular seem prone to the guilt that comes from horses suddenly dying. Often times, these people will seek me out to talk to those animals on the other side. They cry and grieve during the conversation, and I keep an unlimited amount of Kleenex available. It doesn't matter if the horse died six months ago or six years ago; if you do not process your grief it stays with you, like a lump in your throat. A few hours after a session, however, clients come back beaming: at peace and happy with the relationship, knowing their animal is in a great place.

REMEMBER:

1. It is okay to cry and show signs of grief. Deal with your grief honestly so you can move through it. I find that many people don't connect with their emotions, because if they cry, they assume that the emotion becomes a bottomless pit. It isn't. It does seem, however, that the only way to overcome the grief is to go through it. A pet loss is felt as deeply as the loss of a close family member, precisely because they are family members.

2. Don't close yourself off. Connect with empathetic humans. Be kind to your self and avoid people who don't understand. Talk about your pet with family and friends and enjoy your other animals. Look at the information on my website, RosezellasWay.com, about grief.

3. Have a memorial service if you feel one would help. It can help you work through grief and will create an opportunity to allow everyone to share memories of how much they loved the pet. An important feature of any memorial service is that you are honoring your pet.

4. Let go of your pet's essence. Who they are, in love and spirit, will always remain with you and in heaven they can be with you at the speed of thought. Honor them by allowing them to cross over and do not keep them earthbound. (If you plan on keeping your pet's ashes, see the appendix for my ceremony for sending a pet on)

5. Decide if you want a physical memorial to your pet. This could be a tree, a flower garden, or a donation to an animal shelter that engraves their name on a plaque or brick. Remember, the shining star is the years you and your pet spent together.

6. If you need someone to talk to that isn't close to the experience, email me annh@Rosezellasway.com, or AnnMarieHoff@aol.com I can contact your pet on the other side, share how they currently feel and what their truth is about the experience.

7. Only you know when and if you feel comfortable getting another pet. If you let someone talk you into adopting an animal before you are ready, you may make crucial mistakes in picking a puppy or a rescue animal.

8. Grieve within your pack or herd. Other family pets can grieve so deeply that they stop eating and become lackluster. They may wander, looking for the pet that is not physically present. (My cat Speedy wandered for miles: meowing and looking for his passed brother.) The group is undergoing a major transition; make sure you spend plenty of time with them.

9. If someone besides you has lost a pet, meet him or her with tact, patience, and a willingness to listen rather than speak. It can be awkward dealing with another's grief, but it is important to acknowledge their loss. If the person is upset about the circumstances of the pet's passing or seems to be more upset than fits the situation, a gift of a session can be very healing and thoughtful.

Remember, there are always more animals to love and care for. I deeply love all my animals on the other side and yet, Gracie and Lucie have a new place in my heart. I also have the knowledge that I rescued them; to someone else they were throwaway dogs, while to me they are treasure. For all of us, this life together is a second chance.

MEDICAL EMPATH

When I channel a being, I feel how they feel in my body. I can feel nausea, heart palpitations, and diseases I don't know the name of. It is can be very startling. I find myself reaching for the Advil when I am talking to a client before I remember that I am channeling, and it is not my pain. I combine my knowledge of disease states, and am given guidance from the angels and spirit guides as far as the available paths of action away from any illness.

After working with medical intuitive ability for over a decade now, I firmly believe that all illness starts in the spiritual-emotional body, and then if not addressed, manifests in the physical body. Most beings do not know how crucial thought forms are to being healthy. For example, a man saying someone is "a pain in my butt" may end up with a cancerous growth in that spot. My father blithely used to joke that he had "one foot in the grave" only to end his last years with a leg amputation and that leg buried in his cemetery plot. Bernie Siegel (the doctor renown for starting the first cancer support group, and author of many books on living your healthiest life) commented that he could tell within five minutes what type of cancer a patient had just by their language.

Animals that are connected to humans many times have the ability to stand in front of an illness and manifest it. From what I understand, this is a choice the animal makes. It is a choice made out of love and devotion. If the reason the illness has come to the human is removed, both the animal and the person miraculously recover.

I am still evolving in my beliefs on what impact this knowledge may have on illness and disease. I work one animal, one person at a time and see what is true.

DIXIE

When channeling an elderly dog named Dixie, I felt how her joints hurt her. Many dogs are hesitant to let their owners know how much pain they are in, but Dixie was very forthcoming. She came up with a way to compensate for her inability to continue hiking regularly with her family and wanted to tell me about it. As the arthritis had set in, her family became worried that she would get seriously hurt.

Dixie loved to ride in the car, so she wistfully suggested in bits of pictures, that it would be very cool if she could ride along with Sandra, her owner, with the wind blowing in her face. That would be just the perfect thing to give her a happy day. I was amazed at how Dixie had come up with such a logical way to enjoy more time with her mom, and have fun doing her most favorite wind in the face thing, too. Let the young dogs take hikes, she thought. She now deserved to ride in style "with the windows down" in complete and sheer dog bliss!

When doing a session I tune into the vibration of the animal (by using their name) and intuitively scan the animal's body by how my own body feels. If a health issue exists I will feel it. Also, I ask the client to give me the age of the animal while I receive the physical age from the guides. If there is a large discrepancy, (for example, the owner says 3 years old and I get 7) I know that something is going on with the animal that is making them age prematurely.

After I receive this information, I use my medical knowledge to discern what is actually happening. The definition of an Empath is someone who feels what another feels in one's own body. With over twenty-five years in the medical industry and with farm livestock experience, I am usually quick to understand the situation. If I do not get an immediate hit, I ask the angels and spirit guides to add additional information. If I do get a hit concerning the medical condition of the animal, I run it past the guides to make sure I have correct guidance.

When dealing with health issues of your pets, there are a wide variety of professionals you can call. I want to make sure that you know that with a medical issue, your veterinarian needs to be called. However, I recommend that you contact an intuitive as well, to fully understand the cause and to better determine the cure of your pet's illnesses.

I have learned that illness starts in the spiritual and emotional body then, if not dealt with, moves into the physical body. For a resolution of an illness, a complete cure, the root cause, the energy that started the disease in the first place must be removed. An intuitive can give you the bigger picture of why a disease or illness has come to your pet and your home.

HOSPICE CARE FOR PETS

Hospice care (or palliative care) provides many guidelines to follow while caring for your pet at home. The main goal of hospice care is to recognize life all the way to the end and its purpose is to relieve suffering while on this journey. It sees death as a natural part of life and does not fear it.

You and your pet will have your own unique experience with this, because it involves your personalities your hopes your dreams as well as your fears. Hospice care for your pet is the greatest gift of love you can give them; when you feel it is appropriate.

It is acceptable to euthanize an animal in this country if we feel we have reason. With so many dogs getting cancer today (one in four dogs in the United States currently contract cancer) cancer treatment and end of life decisions are becoming more common. As a medical intuitive, I have the ability to help you make these decisions with input from your pet. I recommend you use a pet psychic to consult your pets about their own health care.

A DOG WITH CANCER

How far do you go with medical treatment? A dog named Chad was in constant pain from cancer ravaging his body and he spoke to me about his desires. Additionally, Chad's owner wanted to know what Chad's wishes were about pain medication and dying.

Very diplomatically, Chad asked his owner if he would ever get better, particularly whether the purpose of taking pain medicine and being foggy in the head was to get healthy again. Specifically, Chad also wanted to know if he was suffering through cancer treatment now so that he would eventually feel better at some later date. When he was told that he would probably never feel healthy again, he questioned the point of it all. He indicated that he would rather pass away quietly than spend a prolonged time dying.

Plan ahead, and find a vet that makes house calls. They will come to your home for your animals and help them transition. Know that you will know when it is time; your animal will tell you. I believe we hold onto human life far longer than we should at times, and that hospice care is the more dignified answer in many cases, for pets and humans alike.

Many owners experience guilt over having to make medical decisions for their animals. Learning how the animal feels about their treatment can assure you that you are on the right path. I have found that people often feel worse over a lost pet or an animal dying than they would if it was a human family member. Perhaps this is because we are totally in charge of our four-footed family members care. Humans communicate what is wrong, how they feel, and take ownership of their own health care. I have worked with people who lost animals a decade ago and are still carrying grief, guilt, and regret.

STAN'S STORY

When I was a pharmaceutical representative, one of my physicians owned a dog named Stan who had terminal cancer. At the time, however, we didn't know it was terminal. I did a medical intuitive reading on the animal and shared the information.

Whenever I came to see the doctor, I would ask him how things were going. Actually, in my head I would ask the spirit guides first, and always get, "Oh, the dog's a lot worse."

An ill animal is not a positive, or uplifting topic to discuss. I did express my feelings of sympathy, but I always wished I were in the position to do more.

Then one day I was in to visit the doctor, and I checked in with his dog, and found that he was very blissful and happy. So when I saw the doctor, I said, "You know, Stan is finally feeling better, that is so great." He replied, "Stan died yesterday."

That was my first awareness that animals come through similarly, whether they're on earth or in heaven. Furthermore, a dog will come through immediately after they pass; it doesn't appear that there is a waiting period like with people (There have only been two occasions when I wasn't able to reach people on the other side, and in each case, both of them had died recently. I now know that people go through a life review, and there's a time period where it's not easy to connect with them after they have passed). Animals are present immediately.

THE PARVO PUPPY

I was packing, getting ready for the drive to the Equine Affaire in Los Angeles from Tucson, when it started to storm incessantly. I had been hesitant to leave Tucson, because I didn't have a tarp to cover the items that were in the back of my trailer that I would set up later at my booth. The Equine Affaire is held at the county fairgrounds in Pomona, California, which has a strict labor union. I knew that I had to get to Los Angeles by nine that evening, or coordinate my driving so that I reached Pomona at Eight a.m. when the fairgrounds opened. The weather wasn't getting any better, so I made the decision to leave around midnight.

As I sat down to eat dinner at 9 p.m., I suddenly felt violently ill. I wanted to throw up—even though I hadn't eaten for several hours—then I felt a pain exactly like what I received when I grabbed the electric fence as a child. The shock of electric pain ran through all my bones, up my legs, my vertebrae and back down my arms. The thought went through my mind that I wasn't going to be able to make it to Pomona, that I was just too sick. I put the plate aside, and leaned back on the couch.

The phone rang. As I got up to answer it, I was so weak I didn't make it to pick up the phone in time. I did see the number flash on caller ID; a North Carolina area code, and I knew it was a client. I sat down at the kitchen table, not feeling well enough to stand, and dialed star sixty-nine. The number came back in a dull monotone over the receiver. I tried to write it down, but it sped by. I starred it again. Again, it was too fast. It took me ten tries to get the number correctly, that was how poorly I felt. I felt a distinct foreboding. It was midnight in North Carolina. I forged ahead and called the number anyway.

A woman who had been my client two years previous answered the phone. She gave me her name, Kalen, and I remembered her because of her unique name. Kalen once had cat behavior issues, which were the result of her brother on the other side tormenting her cats. At that time, I did a reading, a clearing, and everything became okay with her cat again. Kalen told me that this time she had a new puppy, and she needed my help.

I knew I was leaving for Pomona in a few hours if I felt better, so I tried to schedule an appointment for her later in the week. I was greeted with silence on the other end of the line. "Is that too far away?" I asked. Kalen responded with a yes, and then blurted out that her puppy had Parvo and wasn't eating. Tuesday may be too late, because he may not be alive.

A light switched on in my mind as I heard the guides saying, "You feel the way the puppy does!" I told her about how I had become sick just a few minutes earlier, and that it must be how her puppy felt.

Galen told me that the puppy had been at the vet clinic for over a week, and had rallied heroically. They spent over $10,000 for the treatment. Now, the puppy was home again, and it wasn't eating. I told her that I understood; that I had just pushed my dinner away because I felt so horrible. I still felt this way, and was having trouble swallowing. I told her that crunching dry dog food was just not possible for her pup feeling the way he did. She asked me what I thought he could eat. I explained that I couldn't think of anything that would feel good. Channeling the puppy's feelings, I knew chewing on anything would hurt too much. As far as her puppy was concerned, chewing was out of the question.

The guides reminded me of a nutritional paste that I used once when a kitten got cancer and stopped eating. I didn't remember the name of it, but the guides alerted me to the cabinet it was in. Even though I hadn't used it in three years, I immediately found it, Pet Gold Super-Cal.

"Kalen," I asked, "have you tried this nutritional supplement?"

"I haven't heard of it, and I would think my vet would have told me of such a product."

"He has to eat something, and this is a complete food that your dog can eat without chewing. You need to try it."

While I continued talking to Kalen, she looked up the product on her computer and found that it was available at a 24-hour store near where she lived. "I found it for sale here Ann, I'm off to get the Super-Cal to save my puppy!"

After I hung up, all the symptoms of illness I had been feeling disappeared. The puppy rallied that night and in time gained weight on the paste, alive and healthy all because of a lifesaving communication.

RUTH AND HER GOLDENS

Since I am an animal medical intuitive, I can feel how the pet I am working with feels in *their* body, which seems strange even to me.

Ruth has a soft spot in her heart for older dogs, especially the ones that have flowing goldish-red hair, brown eyes that shine with love and weigh around 80 pounds. Some of Ruth's goldens come to her as old as ten, often kicked out of or separated from a family they had known since birth. Without personally knowing why each dog was surrendered, I do not understand how someone can abandon a member of his or her household. I find Ruth's love when caring for these Golden Retrievers worthy of God himself.

Because the dogs Ruth rescues are older, they tend to have more health issues. She called me many times to inquire about the health of one of her pack.

One of Ruth's dogs was a wonderful, beautiful golden retriever named Hollywood that was ten years old. He was diagnosed with bone cancer in his leg. The veterinarian wanted to cut Hollywood's leg off; the best way to assure that the cancer would not come back.

Ruth asked me to talk to Hollywood about what course of treatment he wanted and to ask him how much pain he was in.

I greeted Hollywood. He became animated, much like he had done once before when I had talked to him. I asked Hollywood what course of action he wanted to take. He replied, "I do not want any heroic measures," he paused and then added, "But I don't know what that means."

After I said this, Ruth laughed, "He must have overheard me talking on the telephone!"

At first, Ruth honored Hollywood's request not to remove his leg. Later, when cancer seemed sure to take him, she acquiesced and Hollywood had the surgery to remove it. He lived for another year, never losing his wonderful, loving energy.

MIKE'S COLIC

My horse, Mike, has had a history of colic a disease that in some cases, can be life threatening without surgical intervention. Mike had colic surgery in California and I was in Tucson, so I couldn't be with him. Mike is very attached to me so it's difficult on him.

He had colicked once when he was with me in Tucson. I had fed him while I was angry about a conversation I had with the people I purchased Mike from. Mike picked up on the anger and internalized it, somehow mistaking my anger at his previous owners to be about him instead. He nervously ate a whole bale of hay that night, which laid him flat on his side the next day sweating profusely with colic.

After Mike's second surgery, I got a call from the vet in California, that he had colic yet again. She told me, "You know, he's not rallying, so we're going to have to take him to surgery again." After I hung up, dreading another surgery for Mike, I called in the angels and spirits guides and had them put protection and healing energy around Mike. The vet called me back fifteen minutes later, "He just got up and is standing there eating. I can't take your horse to surgery when he's standing up eating hay."

Mike's story is a tribute to the power of love, angels and spirit guides. Never think you are powerless. Expect a miracle. I have found that when you expect a miracle; ninety percent of the time (maybe a hundred percent of the time) you get it, or something even better. Mike is healthy and happy today, and hasn't been sick since, without further surgery.

GRACIE'S SEIZURES

I took my girls, Gracie and Lucie, for a walk one afternoon, and when we came back, I heard a noise while I was checking email. I looked up to see Gracie flat as a board, shaking on top of her food bowls. Panicked, I ran to her, not really knowing what to do. Briefly the seizing quit, so I reached to pick her up. My finger had barely touched her, when she started to shake again. I had adopted the girls a year earlier and I remember looking down at her thinking; "Really? This is how it's going to end with Gracie and me? She's dying from a seizure right in front of me without being sick a day since I've had her?"

I grabbed Gracie and put her in the car on the passenger seat. She was shaking, and still stiff, so I arranged her best as I could. I got in, and turned the air-conditioning on full blast, heading to the emergency animal hospital.

A few minutes after I got on the road, Gracie rallied and sat up panting heavily. I turned both of the air conditioner vents on her, thankful to have her back with me, but still worried at how hard she was breathing. I drove as fast as I could toward the hospital. Right as I pulled into the parking lot, Gracie seized again. She shook violently, and one of her paws struck the gear-shifter and knocked the car into neutral. In my state of confusion, it took me a few minutes to figure out what was wrong and why I couldn't pull into the parking space. Finally I got the car back in gear.

I grabbed Gracie and ran into the hospital. The veterinarian and the techs assessed the situation quickly, and let me carry her into an examination room immediately. They made me wait outside while they worked on her. They gave Gracie Valium in an IV drip and who knows what else. Afterwards, the vet came out to talk to me.

Because we had just walked off leash prior to the episode, I didn't know if Gracie got into anything that might have caused the seizure. From what I was receiving from the angels, I concluded that seemed likely. I could not get confirmation to determine whether Gracie had epilepsy. If she did, would it show up as a life ending seizure the very first time it manifested? Yet quite frighteningly she had quit breathing three times before we had reached the hospital.

Gracie spent two overnights plus another day in the hospital. At home, Lucie allowed the cats to run roughshod over her and sunk into the background like wallpaper. Gracie had another seizure in the hospital. Then the drugs kicked in. The vet's technicians told me how Gracie was whining hoping to get out of her cage.

When she came home, Gracie was so drugged that she walked into walls. I still did not sense that she had epilepsy. So I was hesitant to put her on a lifetime of medication and consign her to a dull existence. This was Gracie, my girl who loved to have her head out of the car window, to stand on her hind legs, to swirl and smile. It broke my heart.

I researched seizures on line and consulted with the guides. What came to me was that I had asked Gracie to watch over Lucie when they were in the back yard at night, telling her that the blame would be squarely on her shoulders if the coyotes made off with Lucie.

Lucie had a crush on coyotes, and during a full moon would stand in the back yard barking at them, which would have been okay if coyotes couldn't jump the surrounding six foot tall brick fence and grab her. She had been grabbed twice already; there was a strong likelihood that she could be killed if it happened again. After Patsy's recent death, a gruesome grizzly death in the jaws of a coyote for Lucie was not something I could bear.

The elementals brought up that Gracie was just a dog, and the responsibility for her sister was too much. It was not fair of me to saddle Gracie with such a demanding responsibility. That fact had crossed my mind before too, so I understood what they were saying and removed that responsibility from Gracie and apologized for putting too much weight squarely on her generally competent shoulders.

Not one to ignore the scientific side of a situation, I also looked into the many reasons that seizures happen in dogs. None of them felt like they fit.

I begrudgingly kept Gracie on the Phenobarbital she came home on, while also looking for other healing solutions. When she first came home, I started her on half the dose of Phenobarbital that was prescribed. I also had a cranial-sacral massage therapist work on her once a week, and I surrounded her with healing angels and elementals.

Most people would not have tried to take a dog off of Phenobarbital once the dog had seizures that were so significant respiration ceased. In fact, my Gracie's best dog friend Gizmo was on seizure medication. His humans had never seen Gizmo have an event, just the evidence of one. The risk was Gizmo could have a seizure while they were not present. A seizure could cause death, or wrack up a gigantic hospital bill like Gracie had.

My dog sitters would not care for Gracie unless she was on Phenobarbital. They did not want the responsibility if Gracie had another seizure, and I understood completely.

When I was in Denver for a conference, I talked to a woman who was an animal medical Empath. She told me that there was extra pressure on Gracie, which caused her seizures, and that she was a really good dog who was trying to do what I wanted. This woman felt that the damage that caused the seizures had been repaired, primarily by the cranial-sacral work. She saw Gracie totally recovering. I didn't mention anything about medication.

The next morning right before the conference started, the same woman walked up to me, and pulled me aside. She told me, "last night I had a dream, in which a message came through from Gracie and her guides. She wants off the medication. She doesn't feel good on it. It is poison you know, right?"

I was happy to hear this. I too, received a message to take Gracie off the Phenobarbital, I even asked my vet about it. But she recommended against it, and seemed to think I was crazy to consider it. "Would you really want to take a chance on your dog having another event and maybe this time it goes on long enough that she could die?" She paused, and then added, "If you are determined to lower her medication, you need to do it a little bit at a time. Be around her constantly then for at least two weeks to make sure she doesn't have a problem."

The Empath that shared her dream of Gracie's message did our family a great service. She strengthened my resolve about stopping the medication, just by telling me the truth about situation. When I came home from Denver, I shoved the bottle of Phenobarbital way back inside a kitchen drawer. Gracie stopped it cold turkey. That was well over three years ago, and Gracie has never had another seizure.

Gracie once again hangs her head out the car window when I drive. She springs to action after a toy; she is my sweet baby of joy. I have her back, which is not only what I wanted for myself but also desperately wanted for Gracie as well.

COMMUNICATION WITH
THE OTHER SIDE

I need only the name of the animal or person on the other side to make a connection to their spirit. I know many Intuitives work with pictures, or have to be in the same space as the client. There is even a practice called psychometry, which is connecting with a spirit from the energy that is on an item.

If I just start a session, and see who is around on the other side, the animals most connected, or with the boldest personality will come thru first. When I work big conferences, I do use pictures if available, because talking to a client every 15 minutes results in many, many animals hanging around my booth, and I need to figure out which one belongs to the person in front of me. The first time I had my animals channeled dozens showed up. Compound that by the 1000 people I talk to at a conference, and it is an energetically crowded booth!

I hope you find strength in these true stories of life continuing beyond the physical death of the body. While your pet may never be with you in the exact same physical shape again, love never dies. Beings on the other side can be with us at the speed of thought: instantly. I have conversations with animals on the other side daily. Our animals are bound to us by mutual love, and that bond cannot be broken.

THE WAITING PLACE

The "rainbow bridge" is a theory that has received a lot of acceptance over the past 20 years. When Patsy died, the vet clinic sent me a card about that: she was at the rainbow bridge. This actually amazed me. When it comes to religion, I am always stunned at what is taken exception to and that which is accepted across all faiths. I am not totally sure what the rainbow bridge is. What the Rainbow Bridge states is that dogs and cats go to the edge of heaven, wait for their humans to die, then they all cross over together:

When an animal dies that has been especially close to someone here, that pet goes to Rainbow Bridge. There are meadows and hills for all of our special friends so they can run and play together. There is plenty of food and water and sunshine, and our friends are warm and comfortable. All the animals who had been ill and old are restored to health and vigor; those who were hurt or maimed are made whole and strong again, just as we remember them in our dreams of days and times gone by.

The animals are happy and content, except for one small thing: they miss someone very special to them, who had to be left behind. They all run and play together, but the day comes when one suddenly stops and looks into the distance. The bright eyes are intent; the eager body quivers.

Suddenly he begins to break away from the group, flying over the green grass, his legs carrying him faster and faster. You have been spotted, and when you and your special friend finally meet, you cling together in joyous reunion, never to be parted again. The happy kisses rain upon your face; your hands again caress the beloved head, and you look once more into the trusting eyes of your pet, so long gone from your life but never absent from your heart.

~ RainbowBridge.org

In my experience, the ideal scenario for your loved one is not the rainbow bridge. Unlike humans, dog and cats are available to communicate with immediately after death. Like human spirits, animal energy is in one of two places, here on earth, i.e. earthbound, or a place of amazing happiness I call heaven.

What happens after we die is affected by our beliefs. Since animals are tied to their humans by purpose, love and beliefs, then if their human *really believes* in the rainbow bridge, it is *willed* into being.

If an animal is allowed to go onto heaven, they can come back, reincarnated in a new body. When a pet is on the other side—heaven, or whatever words you want to use to describe it—they can be with you at the speed of thought. Along with that, they are out of pain and incredibly happy.

There were actually a few instances I would say that the "rainbow bridge" theory was consistent with what I have actually found. In those cases, it was clients who believed in the "rainbow bridge". That belief system created a reality in which their animal, after death, patiently sat at heaven's gate awaiting their human master. This is akin to your dog waiting at the door for you to go for a walk. That's fine for a few minutes, but do you really want to keep your pet waiting for years? Decades?

Since they are waiting for *you* to enter heaven, you are also keeping them from the amazing glory and energy that awaits them there. You are keeping them frozen in time, although you are still moving forward. Unlike heaven located animals, they cannot reincarnate.

ELLEN AND THE RAINBOW BRIDGE

"if dogs don't go to heaven, I want to go where they go."
~ Will Rogers

I had this discussion about the rainbow bridge with a client named Ellen. She worked at a pet store, and had lost both a husband and a son. When her dogs passed, she savored the idea that they were still together here on this side, and that they would reach the entrance to heaven and cross together. One of the reasons Ellen held this belief was because she lived in a state of deep chronic grief.

Our loved ones are always connected with us, no matter what the condition is of their physical bodies. However, when we are in grief, we are less exposed to that connection. The spirit guides compare it to being engulfed in fog. The landmark you seek may be three feet away, but because of the fog you literally cannot see your hand when held in front of your face. When the fog of grief lifts, all becomes clear again.

I convinced Ellen that if she allowed her dogs to cross, they would be able to come back in new bodies and support her again. Until then, they would be in touch with the incredible, dynamic love energy available in heaven, and through them, she would experience it too. When Ellen granted me permission to send her dogs to heaven, she took the first steps to healing and being here, in the present. Fact is, in present time is where all creation lies, along with love. All fear lies either in the past or in the future.

DIGBY'S STORY

I came back from Doreen Virtue's mediumship school, armed with the knowledge that all spirit goes on after death, and that we can communicate with them. I also knew that a pet's vibrations are attached to loved ones like human family members.

One day, I had Patsy with me at a Christmas party at Tohono Chul Park, Tucson. Patsy, who duly believed that there was never a person who didn't love her, would lean out of my arms, backwards, and connect with the heart chakra of the first total stranger she saw.

This time the stranger happened to be Julie, and she shared that her dog Digby had died a week earlier. When I repeated the dog's name, I got a picture of him in my mind, and I also got his physical age when he passed. I felt an odd pain in my stomach, and so I asked Julie if Digby died of something stomach related. "Yes," she said, "Digby had stomach cancer."

I then asked if there were any questions she wanted to ask Digby. She came back with the question, "What is your favorite toy?" Digby responded, saying it was a blue ball-like toy. Julie said no, she didn't think that was Digby's favorite—she thought it was a red bone. Several of Julie's friends were with her, and they asked what was that chewy ball toy, wasn't that blue? There ensued a fifteen-minute discussion about what actually was Digby's favorite toy.

Julie continued, "Is there anything Digby wants to say to me now?" Up until this moment, I don't think Julie really thought I was talking to the spirit of her dog; after all, I was just some stranger she began talking to. I described Digby's age, weight, appearance and perhaps one of his many toys. So I knew that she wasn't ready for the profound answer given to that question.

"I worry about them now," I said, channeling Digby's thoughts. "I feel that I brought all the laughter into the home. In fact, that was my purpose, to bring laughter and light into their home. I've noticed now that they haven't gone for a walk since I've died. That concerns me greatly and makes me think they might not take care of themselves in the same way they did when I was around to remind them to enjoy and experience the moment."

What a graceful and amazing answer. I am still humbled by messages from the spirit; they have a grace that is seldom seen in daily life. It took my breath away, to think that, even in death, this dog was still looking out for his human family. Is that not what an angel is? An angel that comes with fur, a sloppy tongue, an urge to experience and enjoy the world, without delay.

The statement hit Julie hard. "Oh my god, I hadn't even realized we haven't been walking! Digby knows! Digby knows how much we miss him! He had a more important spot in our family than we ever knew!"

She started crying. "We haven't walked. We haven't laughed. Digby used to make us laugh." She broke down even further. She was hunched over;

large wracking sobs were convulsing her body. Her friends tried to comfort her, but she pushed them away. She stumbled to the restroom, where she spent the rest of the night.

I felt horrible—for taking that woman out of her light, fun mood, and sticking her in the middle of a dense and uncontrollable grief. I knew that she needed to process and understand what had happened with Digby, but I also realized it wasn't the time or place. I felt guilty and responsible for her public breakdown, and it was the first of many times I was to be placed in a position of wondering what the best choice was—to share the information or to keep silent.

EARTHBOUND PETS

"We just simply do not have all the words to describe everything we need to describe."
~Emmanuel Book One

Dogs and cats can choose to stay on earth without their body after they die. Misconceptions are rampant about earthbound spirits. There are two main places a being can go when they die: what I would call heaven, or to remain earthbound- in this world. Sometimes, it can be difficult to recognize the difference.

Earthbound beings stay in a limbo (here on earth without a body) that contains their last memories at death. Many people that have earthbound pets take comfort in the fact that their pet is still around. I've heard many accounts of ghost pets getting onto beds at night, being heard padding across a wooden or tile floor, being petted, purring, even barking. The clients who are conveying these events usually want to feel that their earthbound pet is with them, but they do not realize that it is not the most ideal situation.

Living cats and dogs see earthbound spirits. An earthbound dog may be the alpha dog; keeping the role he had when he was alive. Other dogs see him and bow. Clients make statements like, "I want Janie to train my new puppy," even though Janie has passed. They do not know that, spiritually, the dead Janie is actually in the room with them, just without her body.

When working with spirits that have stayed here on earth, I always honor them, find out why they stayed, and I honor that too. Sometimes it can be as simple as, "I want to guard my humans because no one else is there to do my job." My recommendation is to help these spirits move on to heaven, or whatever you want to call the glorious place we and our pets have awaiting when we leave our physical bodies. Many pets reincarnate again in different bodies and come back to the same human. They may even stay with that person for several lifetimes.

A pet on the other side (in heaven) can visit us at the speed of thought, essentially instantly. Earthbound spirits, however, do not have access to unlimited energy, as do their counterparts in heaven. The spirit of a dog will stay with us very easily, all we have to do is want them to stay.

Of all the earthbound beings I've run across, a loyal dog or cat is the most benign. They don't need so much energy that the humans they're living with become sick. They don't have malicious plans or intentions, or any desire to "get even." Many of them simply are keeping the promise of service they have given their master—even after death.

The reasons pets stay earthbound are various. It could be because no replacement has appeared to take on their purpose, the owner has asked them to stay, or they have decided that whoever has come to take their job is inadequate. Staying earthbound could also be the result of an accident that surprised them and they weren't ready to cross. The earthbound state essentially consists of remaining in the same context as in a living state, without a body. Personality is consistent in either situation.

I encounter more ghost dogs than I do ghost cats. Cats have a different outlook on life, and see death differently. Cats easily reincarnate and come back to their original human in a new body.

From my experiences, I have found that if a person holds onto the ashes of a deceased pet, the (pet's) earthbound spirit stays with them as well. In the many years I've been involved with animal mediumship, I have never talked to a pet on the other side that was in heaven when its owner kept the ashes from a cremation.

A pet's owner doesn't knowingly keep their pet out of heaven. Whether it is a thought like, "I want my pet to stay with me" or a physical longing of loss that keeps them earthbound is irrelevant. Many times the owner will be melancholy, because the presence of the animal's spirit prevents them from healing and moving on.

When I explain the circumstances around being earthbound to my clients, they want to allow their animals to go to heaven. It seems that dogs are simply trying to comply with the beliefs of their humans. If you want to send your pet to heaven but keep their ashes, I have a blessing (see appendix) for you to do it yourself.

When a pet is in heaven, they can be with you at the speed of thought. You keep your memories, of your pet as well as the connection. The difference is, when the pet's spirit goes to heaven they are ecstatic. I can tell when animals are earthbound because they're melancholy, or have pain in their body. They're the way they were when they died; only they no longer have a tangible physical body. In heaven, it is sheer bliss.

THE JUNKYARD

Guy was a man with hopeful eyes and a sad smile. He said that he wanted to find out about Barry, a dog that he owned in high school that just disappeared one day.

I tuned into Barry, and felt a dog around 70 pounds, with short speckled brown and black hair. Barry showed me a lot that had a chain link fence around it with three strands of barbed wire on top. There were cars around the lot, in various states of disrepair. In my mind, the picture was shown like a video, while simultaneously feeling how the dog felt. I experienced what he was thinking with combinations of words and subtle impressions.

I could see Barry becoming aware of an old man sitting with a shotgun, bib-overalls on, a scruffy beard and a baseball cap on his head. Barry was lost, and somehow had wandered into the yard, thinking it was a short cut on his way home. He sensed the man's hair-trigger temper and cocked shotgun was not a good mix.

Barry heard the old man snarl, "If you know what's good for you, you'll skedaddle. If you leave right now, I might let you live,"

Under the man's fixed gaze, Barry started moving very slowly, gliding toward the wheeled chain-link gate that was at the far end of the lot. In slow motion, he tried not to make any fast movements or noises that the old man would panic or overreact to. Gaining distance consistently, Barry was only several feet from the gate now, the opening a wide, gaping flag to freedom. I could feel the dog's relief at seeing the gate, knowing that the tight spot was going to be over soon. The old man seemed to not be watching him, absentmindedly trying to swat away a fly, with a bead of sweat trickling down his neck. A slight breeze started, coming from the direction of the gate. Freedom. The wind played on his hair, whispering the way home. Another step. Easy now.

With each step, Barry would hesitate, framing himself like part of the surroundings, still and quiet. Gliding another paw forward, freezing and listening with his whole body to see if the old man had moved. The man's head leaned slightly to the right, the way a head drooped before its owner left the body for slumber. Barry took another hesitant step sliding his paw forward. Pause. The breeze lifted the fur on his face. He felt the sweet bliss of the sun and a slight breeze. A few more steps and he could run. He had made a mistake coming into this yard, he now knew there was no save way through. The apparent short cut was taking more time. Another step. He heard the shotgun click. He was unaware of guns; he had never been around one before. Barry willed himself not to look back at the man and didn't want to move quickly and attract more attention. He estimated how far he was from the gate, five or maybe six steps.

Once he was through the gate, he could cut a sharp right or left and run. He wanted to escape this horrible yard, this awful man, and this whole terrible day. Barry thought of his boy, the love and fun they shared, the days of playing fetch together, and watching over the boy when he met his friends in the park. He knew his boy was very worried about him; he could feel the worry and sadness contained within the boy. Barry knew his purpose was to love the boy, and to make him feel special, giving him something that was totally his own, not his siblings. Barry worked very hard at loving the boy, making him laugh, , smile, and giggle constantly. They were connected, they were family.

Barry had one more step. He was hopeful. He knew the way home. His mistake was taking the junkyard short cut. What was this old man doing with a shotgun? What was he guarding?

Then I felt it. Felt it before I even heard it, hearing it from some far off place, like Barry's ears weren't working. The feeling was unmistakable— even though I have never been shot—a sharp, direct hole that entered his body and came out through his chest. Barry did not have to describe it, because I felt it exactly. Laser sharp, intense sensation, breath ending.

Barry could not understand why the old man hadn't kept his word and allow him to walk out of the yard. The confusion I felt from this dog was immense. The fact that he had wandered in from off the street, yes, trespassing, but it was an innocent mistake. He had immediately done what the man had told him to do.

This was my first experience of how dogs take humans at their word. Dog's brains aren't made with the ability to think that we can do anything other than what we say. A lie is beyond their comprehension.

From what I received from Barry, the only thing he felt from getting shot was the initial tunneling shock of the bullet, but no pain. Barry showed me this, hovering over his toppled body, then whisking away and going to his boy. He wanted his boy to know that he hadn't deserted him, that he hadn't broken his honor. A deep immense misery set in, one of not being able to go home to his boy.

In the end, Barry wasn't able to get home and became extremely upset over leaving without letting Guy know.

Since Barry, I have channeled thousands of dogs. With all of them, I feel the same confusion when humans actions and words are not in alignment. The concept of lying is something that dogs don't seem to comprehend.

The pictures Barry sent me of the yard with the three strands of barbed wire at the top of the fence and the gate on wheels that could be rolled open or shut to let large things through is a place that is very distinctive and does not exist in many residential areas. My first response when I pictured it was that it would ring true with Guy, if the junkyard were in his neighborhood. I described the place to Guy, he immediately confirmed that it was near his childhood home. Since that time, I have channeled many on the otherside, animals and humans alike.

Feelings from Barry jumbled all over one another, coming to me, like hundreds of rubber balls, once locked in a container bursting forth, with different colors, sizes, dimensions and needs. Most expressed a sense of frustration over failing to keep his promise of always being there for the boy who had grown into a man.

Barry became my first experience of a dog that had stayed earthbound, his spirit on earth all the years since it had separated from his body.

THE WANDERER

Dr. Masaru Emoto (The Secret Life of Water) shared that spirits are not passing to heaven, but staying in the heavier energy around the planet. Because of this, the vibrational tone of the earth has become lower than what is ideal. (Lecture, Tucson, AZ, 2009).

A dog-named Jasper came through shyly during a session for his owner, just saying a few words at a time. He talked about a girl dog. One day she walked in front of him, and though he tried to follow her, she only got further away. Jasper was a lady's man, (in a dog's world) and he had hooked up with many girls, many times. He really enjoyed going out and about, looking at ladies, yet he had always found his way back home before.

But this girl was going so fast that he had to focus *hard* on keeping up with her. Then much to his horror he became lost. He was alone in the desert on a hot day with no water. Jasper sheepishly admitted that he'd been foolish; he got lost and died in the desert. He wanted his human to know what had happened to him.

You could tell Jasper had male pride. He didn't want to admit that he had gotten lost, which ultimately contributed to his own demise. Over and over he kept saying, "I had always found my way home before."

Because Jasper still had issues on earth, he had stayed earthbound. My client finally knew what had happened to a loved and loyal friend. His owner consented, and we sent Jasper to heaven.

Jasper had the characteristics of earthbound dogs I have come to know quite well. He was dedicated to his owner and did not think of his welfare, only hers. He was hesitant to say that he had screwed up, while being devoted to staying around. He did not know what year it was, or that much time had passed since he died. He remained in a state of limbo—where time was not only irrelevant it was unnecessary. He also didn't place any of the blame for his death on his owner: instead, he took total responsibility, himself.

For the ceremony on sending earthbound spirits and the recently deceased to heaven, please see the Appendix.

EPIPHANIES

THE SPIRITUAL PURPOSE OF PETS

According to Sidi, a Sufi Master, "If humans only had the five characteristics that God gave dogs, there would be no more war. Dogs are loyal, they protect their homes, and they do not hurt anyone. They have the qualities of trust and surrender, honesty, sincerity, care about the beloved, and cleverness."
~ The Sufi Realities

What is the worth of your dog? Do you consider your dog family? Ninety-one percent of people with dogs have more pictures of the dog in their wallet than they do of any other family member. Does your dog add to your family, to your household? Dogs have a purpose and they like a job. What is your dog's purpose? Do you know?

Many seriously ill people hold onto life because of their commitment to their pets. They don't want their dog or cat to be alone. Many more are inspired by the exuberant happiness pets have. With that being true, they can get out of bed in the morning.

Pets come with a purpose, and they need a job. If you don't give them a job, they may create a job you don't like. It makes sense to give your dog a task that makes your life easier and actually adds to the health of the family unit.

An example of an unwanted profession is your dog barking at anyone that walks past the house. Numerous dogs will create a job similar to what they are bred to do, (i.e., a border collie meant to herd sheep may try to "herd" the cats constantly). As a puppy, my border collie, Mandy, would pull on the ears of my Nubian goat, trying to get the goat to run so she could chase her and herd her. As a result, my goat's ears were shredded. Many working breeds of dogs are meant to work at least eight hours, so a simple walk around the neighborhood is not going to get them to wear out.

How do you show your pet you love them? What part of the day are you and your pet on the same wavelength? Do you schedule time to be together each day? From four to six every afternoon, I walk with my dogs for an hour. That is their time and it is sacred. No excuses not to go. Actually, we've struck a deal: they don't bark during the day when I am working, and we always walk an hour between four and six.

Pets teach us about unconditional love, acceptance and communication. Cats and dogs are like apples and oranges, different but like fruit in the same bowl, can exist harmoniously in the same space. My household fur family and that of many of my clients co-exist as proof. It is not a coincidence when either species crosses your path in life. Both cats and dogs can begin as spirit guides or angels so concerned about their charges that they manifest into physical form. This devotion is truly unmatched.

As spirit guides, they were being ignored, so they solved this problem by coming into physical form as cats.

Cats can rub up against people, or sit on laps and purr. As such, they have the ability to help ground and influence their owners.

One of the cats brought up the subject of meditating to his purr— he could get his human into a meditative alpha wave state with his purring. He was never able to do that as a spirit guide.

Many cats and dogs come into a person's life to help them expand their purpose. For example, my purpose is that of a messenger, to increase people's knowledge of animals, and to transmit messages from spirit. My dog, Patsy, came to me, and helped me interact with people that needed those messages. Patsy had an amazing knack for finding people who needed my help in their lives.

I have encountered pets who exist to support their owners. They do this by having a role in our core purpose, loving us, and facilitating the meeting of key individuals in our lives. They can also manifest our illnesses, take on our emotional energy, and help ground us. They allow us to express a previously untold emotion that resides inside. Pets hold a mirror up to us, allowing us to see ourselves through loving eyes. Pets also introduce us to many people and other animal lovers. I am always amazed at the look people get on their faces when they see a happy dog. Humans' protective armor dissolves and melts away when they see a friendly pet.

Having the skill to channel information from humans and animals has allowed me to know both species better than if I only interacted with one. It has given me insight into comparisons and hidden corollaries. If there are problems with an animal, the root of that problem is usually their human; the pet may be acting out, or carrying the brunt of the emotionally charged atmosphere in the home. It can be very similar to how a codependent family member exists in an addict's household.

MY MOTHER AND THE FARM CATS

The vital function that pets fulfill in this world hasn't been
fully recognized. They keep millions of people sane.
They have become guardians of being.
~ Eckhart Tolle

The oldest of seven sisters, my mother was raised in a family long on responsibility, but sparse on joy. She grew up in the town of Clinton, Iowa. She never shared any stories with me about city life. It was as if her life was started when she married my father and moved onto the farm. When my father wanted to win a verbal argument with her, he would remind her that she had been too poor to even have a bicycle as a child. Those simple words were enough to send her into a prolonged hysterical crying fit.

Both youngsters during the depression, when my parent's married they purchased my grandfather Hoff's farm from the uncle who bought it during the depression. My father believed in the inheritance of land, buying the homestead instead of other farmland that looked more lucrative. Mother evolved into a responsible farm wife, constantly working.

During the seventies and early eighties, our farm was in the top ten percent of farms in the United States for the volume of livestock raised. We milked around 150 Holstein cows and raised 5,000 hogs a year from farrow to finish. My father did not believe in producing Veal (selling baby male calves at weeks old that have not ingested anything but milk) so we also raised calves to market weight.

When the milking was finished in the morning and night, the pipeline would be shut down and drained. The pipeline milk would go into a large bowl, and be carried upstairs for the cats. This was done twice a day. After I moved to Arizona, my Mom started carrying the milk twice a day.

Our dairy parlor was an older set-up, and needed to be modernized to continue in the dairy industry. A new pipeline system was hundreds of thousands of dollars. In the 70's we built several confinement hog housing units, which were also pricey, and it was unheard of to have both a dairy and a large confinement hog production operation on the same property. Also, with milking, someone always had to be there to milk twice a day, and milking is a skill that isn't easily learned. After I left the farm for graduate school in Arizona, my nephews helped my Dad with milking. After they went to college, again help was tight. When the government offered the dairy buyout program, my father sold the dairy cattle.

Years later, the hog markets had changed and the situation was such that my parents sold all the hogs. Day by day, all the livestock was sold. Finally, the only livestock that remained was the colony of cats that had been inherited from my grandfather.

Unlike a house cat, farm cats have an actual job on a farm: to keep the rodent population down. The Hoff farm cats were a herd of around forty or fifty cats, with colonies in the barn, the machine shed and the upper cattle shed. Farm cats are individual beings living at the same address. A cat on a farm has a job; they are soldiers in the war against rodents. The story of the Hoff farm cats contains decades of a long running saga between nature, people and animals.

My mother fed the cats because they were her chore. She did this diligently, but without joy or interaction. Without getting to know them as individuals or as the loving creatures that can heal a human soul. After I moved to Arizona, my mother became the Pied Piper of cats. They followed her when she was gardening; doing odd jobs, or anything that involved her being outside the house.

When she was diagnosed with Peripheral Artery Disease, my mother retired. However she still put on her chore clothes to feed the cats. She always saw the responsibility as drudgery and feeding them became something done out of obligation.

Everything in this universe is created for us to choose love. The kitten in the barn, the old feral cat, the blind dog, the plant that isn't thriving, even the water running down the drain, reacts to our love, our input and our words. We are here to experience free will, and that allows us the choice between a caress or a slap, a loving word or a harsh one.

I wondered why the cats survived on the farm after all the other animals were gone. What the purpose was for their existence? What I finally came to realize is that they represented a simple choice that had been a constant theme in my mother's life: choosing to enjoy responsibility, or experiencing it as drudgery.

Anyone who has ever lived with a cat knows the love, affection and joy they can bring into your life. My mother, however, fed over 40 cats for decades, and never held them or brought one of them into her household. She simply saw them as an obligation; much in the same way she saw raising a family. To her, love was responsibility, a task. She never understood that the cats were there for her to make a different choice: a choice for the enjoyment of love.

My mother was diagnosed with Alzheimer's at the near end of her life. She went from feeding cats in the barn to throwing cat food on the cement in front of the garage. While she still cared for the cats, her care was not as complete as it had been earlier in her life. Raccoons moved into the barn and killed the spring litters of kittens (a horrible truth: raccoons eat kittens). I brought several of the farm kittens back to Arizona with me (including Spike, the cat that is laying by my side while I type this).

When my mother succumbed to Alzheimer's, and moved in with my brother, the cats no longer had anyone living on the farm with them. That's when my brother took over feeding responsibilities.

After mom died, all of the cats on our farm disappeared. Fortunately, I have Spike here by my side, the embodiment of the farm cat legacy.

THE ESCAPE ARTIST

"The dog was created especially for children. He is the god of frolic."
~ *Henry Ward Beecher*

Jake was the first dog I channeled. While talking to Jake, his purpose in Karen's life became immediately. Like all dogs that I've channeled after him, Jake had a purpose, one that included his human owner.

Karen's dog came through to me in my mind's eye as a long-haired white dog of about fifty five pounds. He was her childhood dog. Jake would become lonely when the family left in the morning, so he dug under the fence to escape the yard.

When Jake made it free, I *felt* something. I could sense him running, the wonderful feeling of the wind in his hair and ears. He had the freedom of a dog running down a sidewalk, with sun-kissed concrete under his paws. I focused. This dog wanted to be where life was; he wanted to experience life, to *feel* life. So of course he left the yard and ran, seeing what there was of life to experience.

Karen shared that Jake climbed all over her, licking her face, jumping on her, sitting on her lap. Not only that, he was usually a filthy mess to boot. When he got loose, Jake would run through culverts and drainage ditches that had mud and sewage in them. He would then come back to the house in the afternoon, smelly and dirty, exuberant to see her. He overwhelmed Karen, and she never wanted him to touch her until he had a bath.

Jake's message was direct: "I came on this earth to teach you that love is amazing, regardless of packaging or outer wrappings. In my exuberance I embraced love more, even though I wasn't antiseptic and clean. If anything I loved you more when I was dirty because of the exuberance of the moment, not all pre-packaged, sterilized, and held at arms length. That is the way YOU live your life, from a distance, trying not to get dirty. You want your love and life to come in a pretty sterile package."

Jake had an exuberance that only comes from living in the moment, innocently forgetting everything else. He was a child playing and having fun in the mud, not knowing that mud isn't acceptable. He felt the joy of mud everywhere!

I asked Karen if she had a dog in her life now. She said no. I was shown that she still carried the same attitude about life; it had to be antiseptic. This was causing her to miss out on much of the spontaneous joy of life.

WHY IS THIS DOG SUCH A JERK?

"Sometimes, just talking intuitively with an animal can bring about big changes in behavior.... Intuitive communication is most effective when combined with a training program and holistic health-care practices." ~ Marta Williams, Ask Your Animals

Since communicating with thousands of dogs over a period of many years, I've consistently found that animals come to us with a purpose. Their purpose can be as simple as protecting you, making you laugh or helping you to express your anger.

I was once called in to work with a dog whose owner was extremely unhappy with his behavior. The first question she had for me was, "Why is this dog such a jerk, doing things that I ask him not to do, even though he knows better?" I will never forget the answer her dog expressed. Both simple and profound, the dog's response was, "To help her express her anger."

The owner had a personality that never allowed her to show anger. She had been mistreated, abused, taken advantage of, and called names, and never stood up for herself in those situations. Further inquiry revealed that while growing up, she was repeatedly told that it wasn't "ladylike" to get angry.

Her dog provided her with numerous occasions to express anger, such as tracking mud through the house, chasing rabbits and other crafty but unwanted actions. When I explained to her that her dog was "acting out" because his job was to provide her with opportunities to express her anger, her response was, "Oh, he really does that!" The dog had helped her with anger issues more than any human had ever been allowed to do.

Commonly, pets reflect for us the situations in our lives that may not be the way we would like. It is through the behavior of my animal friends that I've gained insights into human relationships. Working from the perspective that the animal holds up a mirror to their human, and that you are the only one who can change your behavior, I have learned many critical insights into my own soul.

FRANKIE AND LEE

At an event in Tempe, I worked with a Bichon named Frankie. He was concerned about his owner, Lee, who was constantly anxious. Frankie tried to alleviate this and ground Lee by licking her face. It immediately occurred to me that this would work: touch brings us into present time. Frankie shared that sometimes he bounced up and down like a super ball, and the whole family would laugh. Frankie knew he was in his forever home.

Later that same day, I talked to Kara. She sat down next to me, with her two children and her dog. She asked me about a previous dog, Skippy, and he came through from the other side. Skippy said he had stepped in front of an illness that was meant for Kara and that actually killed him.. Then the following came through for Kara from her guides:: "Your children are going to be out of the house soon. You will have nothing, totally resenting the years you put into them. Your current dog Jazzy has come here to support you, and help you comprehend your own personal worth."

The following came through for Kara from her spirit guides: that Kara was still over scheduling herself. If she didn't change, that same energy would manifest illness all over again. Her children were fighting all the while we talked, pushing and shoving each other on their chairs. The obstinate boy shoved the girl onto the ground with a self-satisfied smile.

Then following came through for Kara from her guides: "Your children are going to be out of the house soon, and you will have nothing, totally resenting the years that you put into them. Your current dog Jazzy has come here to support you, and help you obtain your own personal worth."

Skippy spoke about the love he had for Kara, and that he was with her in spirit every day. He said that he would sacrifice his life for her again, and his utmost wish was for her to find happiness.

PETS HOLD UP A MIRROR

"Animals have souls too, and most of us don't know that we have soul contracts with both humans and animals"~ John Holland

Pets may manifest their owner's anxiety, anger or behavior. They may even step in front of an illness that is meant for a human and take it on. Pets hold a mirror up to us, we see ourselves clearly in their eyes, yet their love is still there. That melts our protective armor and opens the heart chakra. These animals are given many gifts, so they can work with us and cope with the consequences of their association with us.

In the wild, animals do not over eat. However, household pets will. Frequently, animals weight is proportionate to what their people weigh. When I walk in and see a heavy dog, ninety percent of the time it's because the owner needs to walk and become active. The human may even be a normal weight, but may need to exercise and have more aerobic activity. In fact, the dog may die if the owner doesn't do it. They commit their lives to us.

Pets will step in front of our disease, thinking they can heal it for us, or carry it for us. They are very empathic. One cat told me he thought his spirit was as wide as the sky, and that he could absorb anything. So he took on his owner's cancer and died. His spirit was wide, but not his body.

LOUISE AND JAKE

I knew Louise for years. I came into the doctor's office where she worked on a monthly basis for over a decade. She was the first person I saw when I entered the office, enthusiastically greeting everyone. Louise was always meticulously put together, almost always in jeweled, festive and happy colors. Through dozens of conversations, she never shared her home situation; married, not married, kids, or pets. Louise, aware of my gift of being able to communicate with animals began telling me about her dog, Jake.

Jake was the joy of Louise's home life, and she brightened just talking about him. She was concerned he was packing on too much weight. Working in a doctor's office, Louise knew the risks involved with being overweight for both species- high blood pressure, joint stress, a heart having to pump more to keep blood circulating in a larger body. Louise made an appointment with me to see Jake one Saturday.

That weekend, I drove to Louise's. She lived in a nice neighborhood, with little traffic on the road and neighbors on both sides. After our initial greetings, Louise and I sat on the couch, with Jake between us. I did a blessing and clearing, then I focused on Jake. His first statement shocked me so much; I almost fell off the couch.

"I think my mother should get a divorce," he said matter of factly, "we would be better off without him." When he said this, I also got his (dog) idea of a relationship—which to him meant leaning on each other, spending time together, loving each other, playing, and having fun. He could not comprehend the financial obligation that people sometimes find themselves in, nor did Jake see any reason to stay together because of once stated marriage vows.

Louise explained to me that she and her husband were essentially estranged, even though they were still living in the same house. Which was divided down the middle, with each living in their separate spaces, so that the only room they shared was the kitchen. Both living rooms off the kitchen had large screen televisions. Louise said they both liked football, but watched games separately because they supported different teams.

They were even split on the pet of preference: Louise had Jake, and her husband had a cat named Sam. Her husband insisted on feeding Sam in a bowl on the kitchen floor. Jake, loving food, would mosey up and finish off whatever Sam had left for later. Even though Louise had discussed it with her husband, he wouldn't budge from feeding his cat on the kitchen floor.

At the time of this session, I was in the early stages off my development as an animal communicator. I was just beginning to realize that dogs came with a purpose specific to their owner. I was also beginning to realize that if you didn't give the dog a job, they would come up with one on their own. Jake had a clear vision of his purpose; to take care of Louise. It was the first time I encountered a dog taking on the health issues of its owner. The way the guides explained it, a dog or a cat can see a disease coming towards their human, and they have the ability to step in front of it and take it on themselves.

Since then, I have seen dogs and cats take on cancer, obesity, respiratory illnesses, and all sorts of things. This buys the owner more time to correct the emotional or spiritual imbalance that is at the root of the disease. Louise surely would not be described as svelte, and Jake was gaining weight right along with her. Louise thought Jake's weight problem was the result of eating cat food, but that had little to do with it. Jake had gained weight so that Louise would walk with him and start a weight loss program for the both of them, getting Louise healthy in the process. This dog was so devoted he would risk his own health.

When I questioned Louise about walking, she replied: "I was walking a lot a few months ago, now it gets dark a lot sooner so I haven't been able to. I've also twisted my ankle, so it hurts to walk. I have to admit that has allowed me to pack on a few extra pounds."

I asked Louise if there was any way she could offset the loss of daylight by walking Jake on weekends or during her lunch hour. She said she would think about it, but I knew from her tone of voice she really didn't have her heart in it.

Louise didn't have the energy or desire to get a divorce. Neither did she want to compromise her financial security. I finally extracted a promise from Louise to at least walk Jake on the weekends. It wasn't my place to argue for anything further.

My job is to deliver the message, without trying to convince the client to act or to explain until the message is comprehended. The information I share has the ability to change lives, allowing people to drop old paradigms and walk into the future lighter and more confident. The truth is a person might immediately understand the message, or perhaps only gain insight years later.

Many people, like Louise, are too entrenched in their lives to get a shovel and start digging out. That is what was so great about Jake; he had no attachment to the "situation.". He would be as happy in the park or a hovel with Louise. The main thing to Jake was that he loved Louise. He wanted her to be as happy and healthy as possible.

Dr. Stephan Hamann, associate professor of psychology at Emory University in Atlanta, showed test subjects images of baby seals and puppies. In those test subjects, their brain scans revealed increased activity in the ventral striatum, the area responsible for pleasure. This research is important, because it proves that you can lift your mood by snuggling with your pet. Leave the self-destructive behavior for another day.

SNAUSAGES AND CHOCOLATE

Dogs have a way of finding the people who need them. Filling
emptiness we don't even know we have.
~ Thorn Jones

Even with all the dogs I talk to, I find each one is surprisingly unique. Many dogs have friends, who can become partners in the fun they have. When talking to two terriers in Florida, they kept yelling to me, "We deserve Snausages! We can't have chocolate, so we should be able to have Snausages!"

I asked their owner what the situation was with the treats. She laughed and said that one of the dogs had allergies, so they could no longer be given many of the tasty morsels they used to get.

"Of course," she replied, "they would want Snausages!"

She shared with me that they had never had Snausages: it was from an ad they had heard on TV. The dogs then chorused loudly again that they couldn't have chocolate. The rule that I've established with the spirit guides is that if something is said three times, I have to share it with the client. So I told the woman about the "we can't have chocolate" routine.

She laughed again, and said that her husband told them on a *daily* basis that they "can't have chocolate!" He would then eat chocolate in front of them every day, and tell them that they couldn't have any (dogs cannot eat chocolate because it can be toxic to their system). In spite of the daily teasing, these dogs were very happy. Their purpose was to bring a vibrant zest into their human's life.

THE DOG THAT HUMMED

Karen sat down, and I intuitively checked in to see who was there. I saw a medium brown dog of average weight. Definitely a mutt. He waited until he had my attention, then he went "Hmmmmmmmmmmnnn." I could feel the vibration.

I looked at him again, waiting for him to say something more. Nothing. I refocused. Again, the dog waited until he had my full attention and went, "Hmmmmmmmnnnn." This perplexed me. The dog did nothing else. I focused a third time. Again, he hummed.

My rule with spirit is that if something is shown to me three times, I have to share it with the client. So I looked at Karen and took the plunge.

"Do you have a dog that is associated with humming?"

She smiled widely, and I felt reassured immediately that I hadn't lost my mind.

"I had a dog called Hummer. My husband wanted one of those Jeeps, a Hummer, and since he was never probably going to get one, we named the dog that."

For some reason, the explanation didn't feel like it was the whole story of why the dog was humming. He could have just said, "Hummer." I refocused on Karen again. "He had something to do with humming."

"Oh yes," replied the woman, "He actually could hum. We were amazed, that we named him Hummer, and then he hummed! How wild is that?"

I had never met a dog that hummed before. I love this about dogs: even though they are all the same, they are all different too. Hummer shared with me his own personal vision and skill he used to accomplish his purpose. He came to entertain, to bring laughter into his human's lives. He hummed with a smile on his face—a living, breathing harmonica. Hummer was a simple dog, fulfilling his purpose with a completely unique gift.

PREMONITION (PREVENTION) OF A BREAK-IN

Sometimes the information I am given prevents things from happening, such as information that I received from spirit when I channeled in an "Angel Therapy Practitioner" class (*Trademark Doreen Virtue*). Because of the information that is provided, alternative choices can be made. Like a head-on collision that is averted by a last minute swerve: then all is well.

This was never more apparent than when I gave information to some local restaurant owners.

Stopping at a gallery that represented my artwork (I am a visual artist) I found the owner, Ted, sitting with a couple that owned the restaurant next door. They were splitting a bottle of wine, and they asked me to join them. I sat down, and within minutes the conversation turned to animal communication, talking to the couples' three dogs and angels.

The information that came thru was a little disconcerting. I saw the couple having a party for their employees at their own home. Not only the employees came, but also the guests of the employees as well. One of the waitresses was dating a man who looked over all the possessions in the house, and decided to come back and rob them. The couple did not have a security system on their house, and relied on their three big dogs to keep a look out and protect the property.

The vision of the future I was given was that the boyfriend came back with poison meat and threw it over the fence. The dogs then gulped down the meat, and died. The fact that the couple owned a restaurant made it apparent to everyone that when they were there together their home was empty. All the boyfriend had to do was make a quick call to his girlfriend, and ask if the couple was working. After he poisoned the dogs, it would be easy to jump the fence, open the house and steal as many valuables as he could cart off. As far as I could tell, the girlfriend, a waitress who worked at the restaurant, wasn't even aware of his plans.

When I spoke of this possibility, that their house could get robbed because they had an employee party there, the husband immediately said, "See! See! I told you, a party at our house is out of the question! We can't do that! This is proof!"

His wife, Kate, replied, "Well, she has described our dogs perfectly. Perhaps it isn't a good idea."

Because of the information I gave them, the party never happened, and the dogs were never poisoned. Personally, I felt like this was a great accomplishment. Somewhere in the back of my mind, however, I felt that they didn't totally believe in what I could do, because my predictions never came to fruition.

A few months later, the wife called me to come to their home to see the dogs. One of them, Kenny, was afraid of hot air balloons because of the noise they made, as well as the sight of them when they flew over the house. He had a fear that made him totally decompensate. When I talked to Kate, she shared some of the statements I made the last time I talked to her dogs. Even though I thought I hadn't made an impression, I must have, after all.

I cleared the energy on Kenny. He was afraid of things in the sky because he had grown up inside a puppy mill, and the sky seemed much more menacing than it ever should have. When the balloons made a loud whooshing sound, well, it was just too much! I assigned angels to Kenny so he knew he was safe. From that moment forward, Kenny no longer panicked when he heard the "whoosh" of the brightly colored orbs in the sky.

THE STORY OF SAMANTHA

It surprises me somewhat that distinct groups of people will have different tastes in dogs, or even different dogs for different jobs. With horses (especially the show horses and hunter-jumpers) there are a lot of Corgis.

Corgi's are semi-strange looking. They have long stout bodies over short legs. Corgis have warm eyes and sweet faces; smiling, it seems. Samantha was the "house" dog for my friends, Kelly and Tom.

Kelly called me about Samantha, her Corgi of many years. Samantha had been a great friend, but had caused herself some injuries over the previous year. She now had a really bad hip joint, and could barely walk. Yet she still wanted to chase cattle and horses, and Kelly knew that every minute she continued to do so could hurt her permanently. Kelly wanted to prevent this in the worst way.

From Samantha's point of view, she wanted to be working, because she had noticed that when anyone on the ranch quit working, they disappeared. Samantha knew that on Tom & Kelly's ranch, you had to have a purpose, and you had to be working. Samantha had picked her job, which was herding cattle and horses. This wasn't a job that her parents really wanted her to do. She was loved for just sitting on the couch next to them, or going for a ride in the truck. But Samantha didn't see truck excursions or couch potatoing as her job. She felt she had to have a physical task to do.

Samantha was stubborn, and she wouldn't give an inch.

I talked to Sam several times about her situation. She felt that she might as well be dead if she couldn't herd the livestock. It didn't matter that she was physically hurting her body. She was accurate about the work ethic of her parents; there were no free rides, if a horse wasn't being used, it was gone. This was something even her parents didn't see at first, but as soon as Samantha brought it up, they realized it was true. It took those several conversations to change her mind about chasing livestock.

Finally, Samantha relented to believing she was valued for her companionship. Tom and Kelly gave in some too, they made sure to compliment her on the fantastic job of riding shotgun she was doing in the truck, and how loving she was in the house. After we got Sam to cool her jets with the bovine bashing, the vet was called in to do cortisone injections into the trigger point areas. This plan allowed Samantha to have several more quality years of life, extending the joy she brought into her family.

RUNNING WITH ZOË AND DAISY

"Because dogs and cats still live in the original state of connectedness with Being, they can help us regain it. When we do so, however, that original state deepens and turns into awareness"
~ Eckhart Tolle

The happiest hour of my day is when I take my two dogs, pick up the neighboring two dogs, and we all walk and run together. Daisy, a Cockapoo with steel grayish black hair, white socks and a blaze, hits the ground something like every quarter of a mile, flying through the desert. She flushes rabbits out of the brush and then all the dogs chase them.

When the dogs are so incredibly happy, I feel like all is right with the world. Their purpose is to create a space for me to choose happiness. Such is their gift, I realize I do not need a luxury automobile, designer clothes, or all my problems solved. For in those blissful moments, my daily circumstances become irrelevant. Then I return to my daily tasks with renewed zest and lightheartedness.

MOM AND SONNY
(RURAL ILLINOIS, 1990'2)

*No matter how little money and how few possessions you own,
having a dog makes you rich."*
~ *Louis Sabin*

Mom had a dog that came to an early demise, and my brother helped her pick out a new Maltese puppy to make up for the loss. Mom called the puppy Sonny.

In the frigid Illinois winter, when Sonny went outside to potty, Mom would tie his leash to the clothesline. Mom was still reeling from the loss of her prior dog that had run into the farm's backfields and had been killed by whatever he was chasing. She was making sure she didn't lose Sonny the same way.

However this became problematic because my mother, with her Alzheimer's addled memory, would tie Sonny up and forget him. He was left for hours, long enough to make him hesitant to ask to go outside at all.

Home for the Holidays, I loved Sonny up. He was an amazing little dog, devout in his purpose to take care of my mother. By making her laugh and being an exceptional companion, Sonny kept Mom's Alzheimer's fog at bay.

I will never forget the look on his face when I left for the airport: up on his hind feet, looking at me over the back of a chair, he sent me the message, "What about me? What will happen to me? I'm not sure I am safe…." I felt his fear deeply, but didn't have an answer for him. I sent him psychic social workers, angels and protection, then left to catch my plane.

Six months later, my mother moved in with my brother, too tired of living on her own. Sonny came along, relieved that he no longer had to carry the burden of taking care of Mom by himself. In turn, he quickly became a valued member of my brother's family as well.

BOW'S JOURNEY

At a conference, Melissa asked me to contact the cat she had at home. I asked her the cat's name and she hesitated. The spirit guides immediately told me that the name of the cat had something to do with the way the cat was marked and the way she looked. Melissa chuckled, and I knew it was true.

She was amazed at my answer, saying that the cat had come from a family that was a victim of the Mississippi River flooding from the year before, and she had taken it in because the family's temporary housing excluded pets. The cat's previous name was Patches, but Melissa renamed her Bow. That was because the cat looked like she had a bow on her face. Interestingly, both names had been given to the cat because of the way she was marked.

With that one tidbit of information, Melissa believed that I was indeed in touch with Bow and her spirit guides. This was fortunate, because the guides were focusing on Bow's original owners, the displaced family that had a rocky road ahead. The guides wanted to help the family cope. They gave Melissa information to stabilize the family, then guide Bow to happiness.

Another wonderful aspect of what I do is channel angels and spirit guides for pets and people alike. Even the smallest blade of grass has angels that whisper: "grow, grow". Talking to Bow and the guides, a total picture evolved for the best possible outcome.

I saw Melissa again a year later, and she told me that Bow was still with her. Cats can be that way. They become members of the household. Bow, a loving feline helped two separate families believe in love and miracles again.

REINCARNATION

DO YOU BELIEVE?

"The gifts you receive from the world of spirit come from perfect love, and it is not necessary to connect them to family history. If one were to become enthralled by such a relationship you would find, much to your amusement that you are born to your children you have married your grandfathers, and you have sired your parents. It would all become so complex that it would be difficult to live out in human terms." ~*Emmanuel* Book II

When I do a session for someone and their animal, I just channel what I receive. It is like the part of me that is the ego or consciousness, is sitting on the sidelines listening to everything that was said. What comes thru sometimes surprises me as much as it does the person getting the information. The more sessions I do the more I understand how the universe works. Thru the years I have come to trust this information, to trust it in a way I never have trusted anyone or even myself.

Immediately with the first year, I learned about earthbound beings, the choices that are made after death. How many dogs that came to support their humans stayed around in spirit after they died, and how pets in heaven were so happy, they were in sheer and total bliss. I honestly do not remember feeling that way to that extent before: the way I feel when I channel a being that is in heaven.

Many dogs and cats too come to enrich, enhance and progress their humans life's here on earth. That duty is not severed with death, and many stick around after death to fill the position they were given. So it didn't surprise me when I ran across animals that were coming back to their humans in a new body, a new story.

I have experienced this firsthand, with my cat Peewee coming back as a horse. It is always so hard to believe the miraculous, but why? Is it too hard to believe that we are so loved that these beautiful beings love us enough to return?

I've encountered pet reincarnation multiple times with numerous clients. It even boggles MY mind it is achieved. But I know if a spirit wants to come back, they ask. They can figure it out: we don't need to know how it happens. There is an energy that loves us; that want us to fulfill our purpose and simply wants us to be happy. Why do we have such a hard time believing that something so miraculous could happen in our lives?

Sylvia Brown,(a well-known psychic medium), looked at people who had birthmarks, wanting to know their source. She concluded that the birthmarks were where the person was killed in a previous life. My past life instructor shared that she had a dog that he'd gotten a cholla cactus in his tongue, which left a scar. That dog was reborn as her neighbor's dog, with the exact same mark on its tongue.

When I first uncovered the link between animals that had passed and the fact that they may reincarnate, it seemed very foreign to me. Who I was in my old life would never have believed in reincarnation. So I researched the topic. I found several other animal communicators in the same spot; they didn't believe in reincarnation but they were uncovering clients who had pets that stated they were reincarnated. Because of this new information, reincarnation is being seen in a different light. I now believe that pets reincarnate at times, and the commitments they make to their humans out of love do not die with their physical bodies.

PEE-WEE, THE CAT THAT BECAME A HORSE
(2000'S ILLINOIS & TUCSON)

Home at the farm for Christmas, I was in the barn looking for cats. To my amazement this little yellow kitten popped out from under a wooden pallet. Cats are seasonal breeders, relying on the length of day to bring them into estrus. Because of this, there are usually two batches of kittens each year, spring kittens and fall kittens. On our farm, the fall kittens had a much higher mortality rate because they came into being in harsher weather. They lived inside the outbuildings, but still dealt with winter weather.

If a mother had kittens late in the spring season, she wouldn't have the time to hatch out a second brood. These fall kittens would appear around late September, to middle of October. I had never before seen a young (under eight weeks old) kitten in December on the farm. The kitten's eyes change from blue to the adult color of golden or green at eight weeks, so it is a reliable yardstick to measure feline age. This kitten was half blind in the left eye. Half of the eye was scarred opaque, the other half light blue.

Cats have rather large litters, so to see one lone kitten was odd. It was a cold winter and many of the cats were sickly. Wooden shelters in the barn contained heat lamps, but this kitten was on his own under the pallets many feet away from the cat shelters. He had no family members to keep him warm. I knew the kitten didn't have the health and fortitude to make it through the winter. My mom and brother were very good about keeping heat lamps on the cats, and they were fed twice daily. However an upper respiratory infection was running rampant in the colony and young kittens were particularly susceptible. When I flew back to Tucson the kitten was with me.

I have fallen in love with thousands of cats. A close hundred stick in my mind and heart. Pee-wee totally redefined how I felt about cats. I was going to call him Pee-wee Herman but Pee-wee just stuck.

The inquisitive kitten accompanied me constantly. On a four-hour journey to Yuma, he crawled into the dashboard of the truck. I flashed on a memory of kittens getting thrown from a truck engine when I was a child, all injured. I didn't want him to fall out on the road or get stuck inside the engine compartment. I wasn't sure if there was a way he could get to from the cab to the engine by crawling through the dashboard. I stopped at a truck stop to ask if Pee-wee could get into the engine from the cab of the truck and friendly truckers said absolutely not. Still, I searched and couldn't find him. I drove on. An hour later, he popped out again, perfectly content from his adventure.

I entice myself to meditate by staring at a candle and watching the flame. That seems easier for me than saying mantras or following my breath. While I was sitting on a blanket watching the candle, Pee-wee marched straight up and put his nose in the flame. He hurriedly took his face out, shaking his scalded nose saying, "Why didn't you tell me, why didn't you tell me?"

Another day while I was taking a shower, Pee-wee was pawing at the shower door. I slid open the glass door and he walked in, getting hit by the water, obviously not liking it. But instead of running out or saying he was afraid, he calmly walked all the way around the perimeter of the shower and back out the door, like it was something he did every day. Again I was laughing. Pee-wee was magnificent.

One night I got home from the mall, about 9:30. I've always believed in cats being able to go outdoors. The belief stems from the fact that all the cats I grew up with were outdoor cats.

I had three older cats that Pee-wee followed and adored. That night when I called the cats in, Pee-wee wasn't with them. I didn't sleep that night, because I knew something very wrong had happened: Pee-wee always slept on my chest. I found him dead the next morning, run over by a vehicle.

I had walked my property with sea salt, blessing it and asking for protection. Anyone that crossed that line couldn't harm to my animals. When Pee-wee was hit he was about four inches outside of the salt line, by the shoulder of the road. I live on a cul-de-sac with eight other houses; he had definitely been run over. If somebody killed a person this way at the very least, it would be considered manslaughter. With the killing of an animal, you don't even get so much as an "I'm sorry." It doesn't seem fair.

After P's death, I flew to Hawaii for an angel therapy practitioner class (with Doreen Virtue). I had five different Intuitives all tell me the same facts; Pee-wee thought I was his mom, didn't know he was a cat, and that he was coming back to me as a horse. None of them knew the most important fact of all: at home I had a pregnant mare.

When the foal was born it had white socks the same as Pee-wee the cat. The foal's left eye corresponding to the half blind eye the cat had was half ice blue. I couldn't believe it. It seemed impossible. So the day after he was born I stood in the horse pen in front of the foal. I said tentatively, "Pee-wee?" Much to my amazement, the baby got on his hind legs and started walking toward me on his two feet. It looked like he was going to put his front legs over my shoulders.

I never had a baby horse act like that acted like that. With the hooves of a 120-pound foal dropped over my shoulders, I squealed and stepped back, all the while getting the message, "I want to be held." This was the same spirit I had picked up with one hand on the farm the year before, the cat that slept on my chest and went with me everywhere.

Perhaps Pee-wee didn't make the best choice returning as a horse. But what I heard him say quite distinctly is, "If I'm a horse, they're so big, no one's going to run me over."

Pee-wee hadn't thought it through. He didn't realize that horses don't get to sleep in a human's bed. They live precariously in their own poop much of the time and depend on others to keep their stall clean. They can't climb and stretch and jump. All of this was not ideal. The first day it rained Pee-wee was drastically upset. "What *is* this stuff?" he implored me. "I can't stand it and it's everywhere!" He was referring to the mud created by the rain.

OTHER ANIMALS THAT REINCARNATED:

I channeled a cocker spaniel on the other side that explained he was coming back to his owner as a border collie, but that markings on his tongue would be the same. He had been bothered that he had so much heavy hair on his ears and legs looking like a mop, and he wanted to be a lighter, quick moving dog. He also liked ears that he had as a border, nice and light but still expressive. I asked his owner if he had a specific mark on his tongue, and she said yes, he had two spots. The last thoughts from this dog to his owner was for his owner to be sure to look for another dog with that specifically spotted tongue.

Recently at a conference, I channeled a parakeet that had passed. The bird shared with me how it felt to be caged, and that he didn't want to experience that again in his next life. In fact, he said that he had came back as an eagle, because eagles may not be around in the future and he wanted to experience "eagle-ness" while it was still present in the world. He also believed in humans, and wanted to add his presence to help the world preserve eagles if at all possible.

I was talking to a dog on the other side that wanted to come back to her owner. Many times dogs look at the other dog breeds, and want to change breeds to have fun the next life. Other reasons for changing breeds are to be able to travel on planes, or to be more athletic. The client I was talking to was a very prominent Golden Retriever Rescuer. The loyal faithful dog on the other side asked a test question; "Can I come back as a Golden Pomeranian?" The dog really wanted to travel and to be able to fly on airplanes. She also decided that she wanted to be a "different" dog, one that would be more of a lap dog and stick closer to Mom. She didn't want to just be one of the many Goldens around my client's house.

However, the answer from my client was a loud. "No. I do not want to adopt Golden Pomeranians. I believe in Golden Retrievers, They are the dogs I am committed to, and work tirelessly to save".

I told the dog it was worth a try. That I could see his points, and thought it was a great idea. The next question he had was that if he waited, would she change her mind. My client was firm on the dog type. Steadfastly loyal, the heavenly dog replied, "I am coming back regardless, just thought I'd change it up a bit".

EPILOGUE

JUST ONE

*"Our emotions and feelings have an effect on the world
moment by moment."*
~ *Masaru Emoto (The Secret Life of Water)*

My first professional career was in medical sales. I worked for several companies, and launched 15 new products to market. Physicians go to educational meetings every week, and the companies I worked for would put on educational programs at nights and weekends. Even for me, some of the information was routine and boring, leaving me wishing I had made a different career choice.

When I was doing my Animal Science thesis, researching "Passive Immunity in Neonatal Calves" my major professor told me that if we had two questions where before there had been one, that meant that our research was successful. I was reminded of that statement when a physician told me of his approach when going to CME (Certified Medical Education) meetings. If he got just one good idea he felt the session had been worthwhile. If you can communicate just one idea, see your fur kid in a new light; or appreciate them more, then the effort has been worthwhile.

The first flight to the moon was the most important one. We remember the first person to the South Pole, the first guys to fly a plane, the first person to "discover" America.

Think of this book in that way. The experiences I am sharing with you changed my life, and become an integral part of who I am and how I work with my fellow beings. Open the door to be closer to your pets. Love them in perhaps a different way. Then what I have wanted to accomplish with this book, will have been achieved.

Namaste.

APPENDICES

CALLING A PET HOME

S tart with the statement; "Nothing is lost in God's world." That is the proof you are starting with. A mantra if you will. Intersperse that statement with the other actions in this project. Sit in the center of your home in a spot where you are comfortable. If you have pets in more than one place (office cats and house cats, for example) choose to sit where that pet would be most familiar. Then do a meditation to center and ground yourself (be sure to see tips for grounding yourself in appendix).

Envision a spiritual tree emanating from your third chakra, roots grounded, powerful, and strong into the earth. Meanwhile, the branches are reaching out in all directions from your upper body (if not a tree reference, use the analogy of a spider web, or a wagon wheel, whichever image you resonate with the strongest).

Next send waves of pure love emotion, through the branches, 360 degrees in all directions. Just like a spider-web, each wave has a string that leads back to the center. See these lines going out to your cat or dog. Know that these lines are very strong, and each one leads directly back to you. Your pet can pick a line up and follow it home to you. Clear your mind and see what visual pictures or feelings come through to you.

Say out loud; "I am sending out a web of love so you (insert pets name) can pick up one of these strings and follow it home to me." Then focus on a place where you feel your pet strongest. Ask St. Anthony, St. Francis, Archangel Raphael, Archangel Michael to help you, or whichever angels and spirit guides you feel comfortable with. This is a great place to ask for the elementals (think pixies, fairies, water sprites, elves, gnomes) to help and be of use. The elementals are the angels for nature and animals.

St. Anthony is connected to the word "find." So when you call on him, use "find" in a sentence. For example use the statement; "Find my cat a way home." Archangel Michael is a warrior angel, he carries a sword and protects. Ask him to protect your pet. You can also ask St. Francis to protect your pet. Ganesha is a Hindu God who is the remover of obstacles. You can call on him to make your pet's journey home safe and uneventful. Keep your communications clear, and add protection with it. Include guidance from traffic and human dangers.

I learned the safety aspect from experience. One client had me call her cat home, however, he was stoned and chased by kids when the cat was just three blocks from arrival. The cat never made it home. Make sure you add protection so your pet returns unharmed.

This works. Trust it!

CONNECTING WITH THE ANGELS

I trained as an "Angel Therapy Practitioner" with Doreen Virtue. She certifies people to work with angels and also helps clients connect with their angels, archangels and spirit guides. The Universe has rules just like a State government does. Angels and guides work for God and cannot do anything without God's permission The only exception to this seems to be when a person dies before they are supposed to. This is why children often have stories about seeing angels when they are in accidents or natural disasters. Paul Perry documented this phenomenon in the book, *"Closer to the Light".*

Many adults also have had experiences from being in car accidents where time slows down, and if they do not actually see an angel, they report a sense of peace and calm, without feeling afraid of dying. Our angels exist in a dimension that is always present and available to us. Whether we choose and connecting with them becomes a matter of opening ourselves to them. Prayers are always answered, but sometimes not in the way one would expect.

I once had a client that did computer dating and all five men she went out with had physical birth defects. If you know anything about statistics, this is virtually impossible. The angels told me that the client had asked for men that were "not perfect". It seems like her last relationship was with a very attractive man, and she preferred not to experience that again. However, the Universe took it one step further, and gave her men that had physical defects. This is a pertinent reminder to be careful of how you word your prayers. When you ask for abundance, specify or you may get mosquitos.

Every day for three months, I stated that "I hear my spirit guides and angels loudly and clearly."

Then one night, I came home and a white owl was sitting in front of my carport. He stared at me across the car hood, then flew under the roof of my house. I checked the next day. There was no place for the owl to have disappeared to.

In the spirit world, owls represent wisdom. After seeing the owl I began hearing both spirit guides and angels. That was truly a life-altering day for me. The reason I am sharing this event is that I did not ask just once or twice to hear angels, but I asked *every day for three months*. I also did not simply pose a question. I claimed my power, by saying, "I hear my spirit guides and angels clearly and loudly".

Some things take longer than we expect and we may become discouraged. We might tell ourselves, "Oh, I didn't really believe in that anyway." Abraham the being channeled thru Jerry and Ester Hicks says that all those dreams we have asked for and then cancel were almost to us, and are orbiting around the earth.

Perhaps it took me three months because I never believed strongly enough that a link to spirit and angels were possible. Perhaps my lack of conviction was interfering. I needed to get out of my own way, which I did. I spontaneously began to feel and sense their presence. I tell you now with certainty; angels and spirit guides do exist, and we all have them.

Many people's guides are like the Maytag repairman, bored senseless, waiting for a call from you. We all have God within us. We co-create our reality with the Universe. If you have emotional baggage with the word God, substitute the word *life*. Angels work for God. They are not out there moving aimlessly, doing whatever, they are working for us. Since we have God within us, the *angels work for us!* That means that they need to be given work, they don't just automatically decide to start cleaning the house for you. You have to ask them for the house to be cleaned!

My experience of angels and spirit guides in my life is that they make the path much smoother, and synchronicity becomes an everyday experience.

Once you make contact, you *know* you are never totally alone, and that help is always available (unless, that is, you *ask* to be alone, and then they have to leave).

If you have a physical reminder of an angel in your home, it brings your angels and spirit guides one step closer to helping. That makes angel sculptures and plaques a great house-warming gift, graduation present, or moving out of town gift. I like to have angels where I will see them throughout the day: a reminder to contact them and talk to them. If you do the same, be prepared to see your life transform.

DIFFERENCES BETWEEN A VISITATION AND A DREAM

As a medium, I want to share with you all that you can visit the other side (Along with the spirit energies that are there- like your deceased dog) in your dreams. A visitation is different from a dream because you remember it years later as vividly as the morning you woke from it. This is a non-threatening way to meet and share the love with those on the other side that still connects you both.

BLESS THIS HOUSE GUARDIAN ANGELS

Ask your Guardian Angels to bless your house. *(I recommend having a physical representation of an angel that reminds people in the house that angels are present. Many angels tell me because there is an angel figurine in the house they are allowed to come in and do their magic.)*

Your Guardian Angels are here to guard and protect all that dwells in this establishment. The Angels will answer all requests, prayers and statements made. Be aware of how you verbalize your belief system and your prayers. Make sure it positive, in present time, and not fear based. (A fear based prayer would be: "Please don't let the tornado hit our house and take everything, including our lives).

As living beings, we all have God within. A metaphor for this to think of God is a gigantic apartment building, with each person is an apartment within that building. Angels and guides work for God; and since humans have God within they work for us. My unaware belief had always been that angels were above humans, in the same category as God, up there in heaven.

Think of yourself as the quarterback on a football team, the Angels and Spirit Guides as the other players on your same team. You can pass the ball, in fact that is the way you realize your victory. This example works to illuminate how you have access to a team, yet run the decisions and plays. You are not constantly responsible for the ball.

Instead of requesting something that you don't want to happen, express in a positive way what you do want. Every thought is a prayer, and all prayers are answered. Grace and gratefulness is always the best way to approach topics.

A PRAYER FOR THE GUARDIAN ANGEL

"Bless this house; keep all within safe, vibrant, and aware of their divinity and gifts. Grant them the strength and support to follow their dreams, to choose joy and peace instead of fear. The Guardian Angel will help all within this house without being asked individually to come to their aid. The Guardian Angel has permission to help all that dwell within, and of course it shall."
Blessed be!

HOW TO SET UP PSYCHIC BOUNDARIES FOR YOURSELF AND YOUR PETS

The boundary system you set up for you and your pets is like the firewall for computers. The boundary protects against unwanted energies getting into your system. Not having a firewall is like not having an outside wall to your house. Not having a psychic boundary allows energies to move into your field and even attach to you or your pets.

Ask the Guides to set a 360-degree boundary around each one of your pets. Make sure it is a complete circle around them. Then you want to make it impenetrable by any force that is not for the beings (you can use this for yourself, your children, your pets, or a friend that you are worried about) highest good.

The prayer is this: (to be said out loud): "I am ordering the part of myself that knows how to do it to surround me and each of my pets (say their specific names) with a 360 circle of white light, pink light and golden light. Then place a semi-permeable membrane around it all that only allows in what is for the highest good." Love will always be able to be inside your boundaries.

A current practice is to "shield yourself". This is problematic. Because a shield has an end to it, energy can always get underneath it and lift it. If you are dealing with particularly dangerous, evil or malevolent energy, you may want to add a layer of mirrors facing outward, so that anything sent to you is reflected off the mirrored surface and goes directly from where it came.

Another option is to set mirrors facing inward around an unwanted being, so that any energy, or lack of it, that they give off is reflected immediately back to them.

Some beings cannot create their own energy and attach to others to have power. When I place my boundary, I also state: If anyone is feeding on my energy (or my pet's energy), make it poisonous to that being. That just keeps them off of you without any further drama.

Ground yourself and your pet by saying your specific name as well as each of your pets' names three times, then imagine a grounding cord coming from your root chakra (the area at the end of your backbone) going down into the earth and tethering you to the center of the earth. Vision this for each pet you are protecting.

This grounding & protecting technique works, and works very well. Many of my clients have had dramatic changes in their lives by doing this simple procedure every day. It is good to tie your spiritual ceremony with something you do everyday, like brushing your teeth, showering, doing dishes, running or exercising. Think of it as necessary maintenance for your spiritual body, just like a bath, shower or vitamins are necessary for your physical body.

CEREMONY TO SEND EARTHBOUND SPIRITS AND THE RECENTLY DECEASED TO HEAVEN

Information and Items needed before heaven ceremony is performed:

1. The name of a person in heaven who would come down and get the pet. Preferably a deceased human family member, or good

friend. Most people can think of the name of someone in heaven. The best possible candidate is, of course, someone who knew and loved your pet.

2. The name of spiritual beings that will participate. I use St. Anthony, St. Francis, Jesus, Archangel Raphael, and Archangel Micheal. All are great with animals. Ask for Spirit Guides that you are familiar andl feel comfortable with. I was raised Presbyterian, but have found the Catholic Saints do a great job, so I use them. Jewish clients have asked for Abraham, Sufi's use Rumi or Hafiz and Hindu's have Ganesha, Krishna, and many others.

3. For a group ceremony, have a story or memory of the pet to share: this is completely optional. I have found when you have loved ones gathered; sharing memories is helpful and soothing.

4. Method of disposal of body, if hasn't already been done (This ceremony can be done after body has been disposed of).

INSTRUCTIONS:

Below is the text of a passing to heaven ceremony that I have given. The words can be adjusted so you can make it your own. This can be done when you are by yourself, or with a group of family or friends that knew your pet.

TEXT OF CEREMONY:

"We have gathered together today to say goodbye to the spirit of (name of pet). I am asking for a few moments of silence, during which (name of pet) has the opportunity to share with those present experiences that defined (name of pet) life on earth.

Does anyone present want to share a memory? Please acknowledge the love, laughter and joy that (name of pet) brought into our lives, allowing (name of pet) to comprehend that (his or her) impact on our lives was life affirming.

After everyone willing to share is done describing his or her experiences continue with:

"Realize that though (name of pet) has dropped their body, the spirit continues. Because of the love for (name of pet) we are releasing them to Heaven"

Then say the following:

"I am ordering the part of myself that knows how, to do the following; "I am now asking (insert names of spirit guides that personally have meaning to you per prior examples) along with (insert heaven-based loved one) to come down from heaven to meet the spirit of (name of pet) and take (name of pet) back to heaven with them. I am asking for this to start now, and continue until complete. I am asking for (the family member/friend in heaven) so that (the pet) knows that they are returning to the perfect loving light of God, and are joining loved ones in heaven. I now release the spirit of (name of pet) to the loving spiritual beings that have come to escort (name of pet) to heaven. I am asking for his process to start now, and continue until all are enfolded in the loving warmth of God in heaven."

"I turn over to God all information that isn't for our highest good that is involved with my relationship with (name of pet). This includes but is not limited to; (our/my) sorrow, grief, frustrations, guilt over the way (name of pet) passed to the other side and anger over the circumstances. I am asking for forgiveness and the karma balanced, and that all negative situations that are funded by present time energy are surrendered to God."

"I ask that God look at this evidence at his big desk to the total extent of Universal law, and all evidence held by everyone is released to God so that he can make an informed decision. I understand that only God has the ability to judge events here on earth. I release all judgment, anger, and incorrect thinking I have about the situation to God. I realize that there is perfect order in God's world, and though I do not see it now, there is a divine plan in the passing of (name of pet)."

"I am asking for angels to intervene, and help all that are not at peace with the situation. I ask they be given the comprehension that the love of God will resolve the situation, so no energy is spent bringing past negative memories into the present time. I ask that everyone here knows and feels the love surrounding us. I completely let go of (name of pet) and thank (him/her) for the gifts shared."

This next part is optional:

"I am asking that all who think of and remember (name of pet) remember most what is truly real, the love that (name of pet) came to give and share with us, and the laughter, joy and companionship they have brought into our lives. I let go of all energy involved with (name of pet) for I know that in heaven, there is no time, space or fear so (name of pet) can be with us at the speed of thought. I am releasing (name of pet)'s spirit to the light of God, so that they are again on their spiritual path, and can return to me in another body if it is the pets and God's will.

Love returns to love. Love is real, it endures beyond the wall of death. Any negative energy will be dissolved in the light of heaven. I am grateful beyond measure that (name of pet) came into our lives, and I thank God for the joy, grace, beauty (fill in your own adjectives), laughter, peace and security (name of pet) brought into our lives."

"I know that love, joy, and gratefulness are the highest emotions available to us. I thank (name of pet) for bringing those lights into our lives. I ask that they go with joy and peace, not worrying about those left behind on the earth plane. I assure (name of pet) that their earth family will be well taken care of, and the love the (name of pet) shared remains a legacy, leaving all of us more capable to withstand loss, more capable of easy laughter, and more aware of genuine unconditional love. (Again, add humor or own adjectives)."

The most important issues are: that energy is released, no one is carrying needless guilt, and the soul is in heaven. The end of ceremony is great time to bury the body, dispose of ashes, or bless the urn holding the ashes and set it in a place of honor.

CLEARING ENERGIES

The world you live in is created by thought. The Bible states: "in the beginning, there was the word". It does not need to be said, just thought for fleeting seconds to be effective (Conversations with Abraham, Ester and Jerry Hicks, says 17 seconds).

Clearing energy is something I do with almost everybody and just like taking a bath, most everybody looks better and feels better afterwards.

When doing energy work with animals that are in shelters, found, lost, abused or adopted from one family to another, the most productive, efficient, healing and loving act anyone can do (after providing food and water and getting them out of a situation that is questionable) is to clear their energy.

For the human, whatever positive truths you have, negative underlying beliefs often act as obstacles to you believing that truth. For example, you may state, "I am beautiful." Immediately a small voice answers in your head, "But in fifth grade Stewart told me I was plain and unattractive." This is the underlying belief that you have held onto rather than you are beautiful.

You claim, "I am healthy, vibrant and happy". A voice in your head responds, "You have MS, how can you be healthy? How can you be happy with a chronic illness?"

Animals do not have these programmed beliefs, and so they move into the present moment and let go of fear so much easier than humans do.

However, in *"The Secret life of Water"* Mr. *Masaru Emoto* showed that water responded to negative words by creating a malformed cancerous crystal. When exposed to great music, words of love, the water formed crystals that were magnificent. So don't count on the fact that your animal doesn't know the specific words you use. If you are using negative toxic words, the animal will feel it. After all, bodies are primarily water.

If you tell your dog, "You are such a happy dog!" the dog wags his tail to thank you and supports this idea. Likewise, if you tell your dog, "You are a miserable, disgusting mutt!" your dog thinks, "I am no good." Emotions are like watercolor washes they can affect everything in that painting.

ENERGY CLEARING CEREMONY FOR ANIMALS

"I am ordering the part of myself that knows how to do it, to clear the negative energy in all seven chakras and the aura of (insert animals name and the owner's last name). I am asking that Universal law enforcement take any energies, emotions and memories that have to do with (name of animal) being abused, hurt, attacked, afraid, unloved, or

uncared for and turn those over to God.

I then ask for that information to be scanned for anyone who has done harm to (name) that led to those resulting emotions. Those people or institutions are to be turned over to Universal law enforcement, held accountable for their actions, and prosecuted to the utmost full extent of the law. I am then asking for all karmic energies between all beings and (name of animal) be balanced and brought to neutral."

"I am asking that this procedure start now, and continue until complete. I am assigning twenty psychic social workers, 100 universal law enforcement agents (the number here is yours to chose- whatever you feel the situation calls for) and ten elementals to make sure these actions are carried out to the full extent of the law, and goes through all bodies, all space and all time."

"Once the karma is balanced and harmful energies are removed, I am asking that the space where these energies existed to be filled with a paste of white light, love, happiness, joy, trust, peace. It is your prerogative what elements you would like to place here. It could be love and trust of the present owner or love and trust of all people..

Your animals are on your team also, that is what their purpose is about, that is why they came to you specifically. After doing the clearing I say out loud to my guides:

"I hear my spirit guides and the spirit guides of my pet

loudly, clearly and concisely. I am giving them permission to create miracles in our lives, and I fund them to do that physically spiritually and emotionally."

By saying this, you have given your guides leeway and permission to bring through the special things they can do for you. It also gives them overall permission to build trust with you. Today I trust my and my pet's guides much more than I did even a year ago.

With lost pets, sick and injured pets or dogs in shelters, I also add this statement: *"Make (Name of the dog)'s energy poisonous to anyone who tries to feed on it."*

That will take care of the energy vampires, earthbound spirits, people or other animals that are draining or absorbing their energies. Other than this, I do not focus on the noises that go bump in the night. I took something that I heard John Edwards say to heart. He said "I stand in the light of God, it is all about me and around me, and anything else has nothing to do with me" I move unknown energies to their right and proper place with the help of the spirit guides, but I do not stare at those energies. I will take care of the ghosts that are making an animal's life miserable. This aspect of intuitive work, this preventative step will keep you from having to define it any further.

After you have done the clearing, spirit guide salutation and karma balancing, the next step is to put protection around your pet. Again, there are many ways of doing this, but I have found that this works for me. I am a very sensitive Empath, and so have worked for years to find the proper balance of shielding and energy.

Note: *I urge you to say the word "boundary" instead of "shielding". A boundary is an unbroken 360-degree circle around yourself or your pet, a shield is something that has an edge and can be slipped under or over. Most practitioners will mention a shield, and I have found a shield to be lacking because they have an end that can be picked up and gone under.*

Encircle your pet with what light feels best for them. White light is primarily to heal, so it has the property of making one less accessible to other people. There are days you may want this for yourself and your pet.

Doreen Virtue recommends pink light to make you more accessible. I am currently using white light, then pink light, then gold light. I have seen practitioners use rainbow light or purple light; it really depends on what and how you feel and what you are trying to accomplish.

Just as we are surrounded with an aura, we also are encased in a vibrational field. We are born at a certain speed that can be raised or lowered depending on our companions, what we are thinking, and how we are acting. I ask for my vibrational core to be at God speed, giving me a buffer of space, then I ask for the outer vibrational space to match the vibration of the person I am interacting with.

This is not as important for your pets as the light boundary, but I mention it in case you have a person in you and your dog's life that you feel threatened by and cannot, for whatever reason, disentangle from.

I put protection around myself, and simply add my pet's names when I do this. Attach this exercise to something you do everyday, like brushing your teeth, taking a shower, or walking your dogs. It cannot be measured how much this makes your pets safer and happier, but I feel it is one of the reasons that dogs and cats that I look for are found safe and unharmed. It doesn't cost any money, and you will feel the results when you clear and protect your energy. It takes mere seconds to add your pet's names to the exercise. You can also add anyone you want to be safe including your spouse or significant other, your friends, and your children.

BLESSING AND SANCTIFYING A SPACE

You move into a new space, a person moves out of an existing space, guests come and go; residue energy builds up over time. It is recommended to clear the space and bring the energy up to date. This can be done by you, and is really quite simple.

There are three separate steps to take. The first is to clear any negative or harmful energy that currently exists in the house. The second step is to bless the house. Then the third and final step is to set a boundary so that negative forces cannot enter.

You will need:

A bundle of sage for smudging

A lighter or matches

A shell or small dish to hold the ashes

Sea salt

These items can be purchased at a health food store or wide range of products grocery store.

You want to write the Blessing on paper so that you can say it easily when you are smudging. The Blessing can and should be individual and personal to your specific situation. Exclude negative wording. For example, omit the wording, "I don't want any robbery here." Change it to: "Only people who enrich my life abundantly and peacefully may enter here."

Tip: The Universe doesn't see or recognize negatives or double negatives. Here are two visualizations to help you see this. First, working with a dog. You say to the dog, "Don't sit, don't sit." The dog hears, "blah, blah, sit. Blah, blah, sit". Even though you are telling the dog the opposite of sit, he only recognizes "sit" and so that is what he does. The other is to think of the situation in a visual picture. When you think of the lack of or the absence of something, you create a picture in your mind of that thing. Therefore when that picture exists in your mind, you vibrate whatever it is into being. The "not the vibration of the thing" doesn't exist. You either have the vibration, or it isn't present.

Include in your blessing: "Only people for my highest good may enter here and cross these thresholds". When I first did this, I was in for a surprise. The man that I was dating called with a flimsy excuse not to make our date that night, then didn't show up for the date the next night, not even bothering to call. I realized that he wasn't for my highest good, I had been dating him for something to do but it wasn't growing. Other companions that weren't for my highest good didn't come around any more either.

People, who cut negative thinkers out of their lives, know firsthand how hard and messy the process can be. If you confront someone who is negative, it is highly likely they will disagree with you and you will still have them in your life but now they are angry and pissed.

Instead, when you bless your space, state your desire to attract like-minded souls. Then you will experience a dropping away of situations and people that are not for your highest good. It happens very smoothly, cleanly and quietly. I recommend this choice.

Perhaps you are a lucky one and do not have any negative people in your life and so this point is mute. If so, you are, indeed, truly lucky, because it is a current fact that 80% of human thought is negative.

If you are related or married to a negative thinker start to put boundaries on their behavior. Set a three-minute limit on their discussion about negative issues, and then ask for a positive solution. The question I always ask people in these situations is, 'what are you supposed to be learning here?"

When clearing a spirit from the space, make sure to include the energies of spiritual realms. Say something like this, "All spiritual realms are blessed, cleansed, and cleared, and only energy with my highest good may be allowed to stay. Please fill any space left by removal of these lower energies with the peace, light and love of God."

TIP: If you have trouble with the word "God" (some do) you can replace "God" with the words "spirit", "light, or even "love".

Examples of text to put into your statements:

To clear the space; "I am ordering the part of myself that knows how to do it, and I am invoking help from my spirit guides, to clear all energies in this space that are not vibrating at Godspeed, and that do not have my best interests at heart."

For wealth; "this space creates financial abundance." Or something that rhymes. One client uses, "Life is sunny because I make so much money."

For Peace; "May all that enter this space be calm, joyful, peaceful and create an atmosphere of abundance and peace."

To attract love; "Please clear all energies that are not for my highest good and fill this space with the light and love of unlimited joy. This space attracts only love, joy, and the Christ consciousness energy."

For spirit energies; "If anyone is here that is not for my highest good please have them go to their right and proper place where ever that may be."

It is best to compose your own blessing, because only you know the exact issues you want to address. These examples that are given, are just that; examples. If you feel strongly that you want to add something to what is stated above rather than compose a totally different blessing, by all means do. The blessing is as important as the fact that you are doing it

You have your blessing. Next light the sage bundle, let it burn a few minutes, and then snuff it out in the bowl or shell you have. After you do this, you should have a sage bundle that is smoldering. That is the way a sage bundle for "smudging" looks. If there are a lot of little bright red embers, smash it again, because those red embers have a tendency to jump off and burn things in your house. You want the sage smoldering enough that so that it doesn't go out while you are performing the ceremony.

Carry the small bowl or shell with you during the blessing ceremony. Start at one end of the house, and work your way through each room, saying your blessing at least three times in each room. Open closets and smudge the area's there, and say the blessing once.

Walk around the perimeter of each room, waving the sage so the whole room is touched by sage essence. Rest the sage bundle in the bowl/shell when not in use. Work your way through the whole house in this manner. If you do not occupy the entire house, ask the other occupants for permission to sage their space.

If sage smells too much for you, there are odor free clearing alternatives. This may be a consideration for you. I went to a massage therapist for several years before I was an intuitive medium. I was the first client of the day. I was working in scientific medicine then, and didn't know anything about sage. I didn't know why you would use it or how it smelled.

I walked in his office, and definitely knew something was amiss. What it smelled like to me was marijuana! I mistakenly thought the massage therapist didn't respect me, and was getting high before he saw me in the morning. On top of that, I never said anything to him, and thought this about him for many years. It wasn't until I started using sage myself, and smelled its unmistakable scent, that I realized I was incorrect. Take note of this, and make others using the space aware of what you are doing.

Once you have totally gone through the space, ask for the highest good for all concerned, and thank your guides and God/ spirit/light/love for the assist. Put out the sage by smudging it hard again in bowl several times. Leave it in the bowl to make sure that the smudge bundle stops burning. You are now done with it for this clearing.

For the final step, get your sea salt. You use your blessing with the sea salt also, the part that is exclusive and protective. You have just cleared out any negative energy, psychic build-up; strange factors that you may not even have known were present. With the salt you are going to establish a boundary, so that only what you want in your space may come threw in the future.

With the salt spread a clean line on the thresholds, which means doors and windows. Spread the salt outside the house, at the bottom of each of the doors and the windowsills. It does not matter if the salt is swept away in a few days, the sanctity of the blessing will hold for several weeks to a month or two, depending on what is at the boundary asking for admittance.

If you are worried what people will think if you have a line of salt across your thresholds and doorways, make your line discreet and as fine as possible. The important thing about the line of salt at the door is that it is uninterrupted. Put it in by the door jam, and if people ask about it, tell them you are keeping out ants. (That is if you do not feel comfortable sharing the real reason for the salt).

If you have animals and pets outside the house to protect, walk your property line with salt. I did that five years ago, and have not had a pet hurt inside the line since. I replace the line on a yearly basis, and if I had a higher level of vulnerability, I would spread salt more often.

APPENDIX 8
PEE STICK POTTY TRAINING

Pee Stick Potty Training is a technique that works. Get a stick that is long enough to keep your hands out of urine when your dog pees on it. The stick should be short enough that you can put it in the trunk of your car or behind a door. Take your pup for a walk, and put the stick in the stream of urine when the pooch urinates (or have another dog urinate on the stick).

When you walk your dog again, bring the stick along. When you get to a place you want your dog to do his business, pull out the stick and let your dog sniff it. The smell of urine will remind him that this is what you want done. You know, how dogs sniff everything, and then pee on the best scent? Use that to your advantage.

Even the youngest dog will get the idea that you want them to urinate in the location you have the stick at. Once this happens a few times, your dog will get the correlation between the stick and your desire to have them pee outside when you go for a walk.